Old Spookses' Pass, Malcolm's Katie, And Other Poems

Isabella Valancy Crawford

In the interest of creating a more extensive selection of rare historical book reprints, we have chosen to reproduce this title even though it may possibly have occasional imperfections such as missing and blurred pages, missing text, poor pictures, markings, dark backgrounds and other reproduction issues beyond our control. Because this work is culturally important, we have made it available as a part of our commitment to protecting, preserving and promoting the world's literature. Thank you for your understanding.

OLD SPOOKSES' PASS

Malcolm's Katie,

AND

OTHER POEMS,

BY

ISABELLA VALANCY CRAWFORD.

— AUTHOR OF —

A LITTLE BACCHANTE, OR SOME BLACK SHEEP,
ETC., ETC., ETC.

Entered according to the Act of Parliament of Canada, in the year eighteen hundred and eighty-four, by ISABELLA VALANCY CRAWFORD, in the Office of the Minister of Agriculture.

TO

JOHN IRWIN CRAWFORD, Esq., M.D., R.N.,

THIS VOLUME

IS AFFECTIONATELY DEDICATED

BY HIS NIECE

ISABELLA VALANCY CRAWFORD.

OLD SPOOKSES' PASS.

I.

We'd camp'd that night on Yaller Bull Flat—
  Thar was Possum Billy, an' Tom, an' me.
Right smart at throwin' a lariat
  Was them two fellers, as ever I see;
An' for ridin' a broncho, or argyin' squar
  With the devil roll'd up in the hide of a mule,
Them two fellers that camp'd with me thar
  Would hev made an' or'nary feller a fool.

II.

Fur argyfyin' in any way,
  Thet hed to be argy'd with sinew an' bone,
I never see'd fellers could argy like them;
  But just right har I will hev to own
Thet whar brains come in in the game of life,
  They held the poorest keerds in the lot;
An' when hands was shown, some other chap
  Rak'd in the hull of the blam'd old pot!

III.

We was short of hands, the herd was large,
    An' watch an' watch we divided the night;
We could hear the coyotes howl an' whine,
    But the darn'd critters kept out of sight
Of the camp-fire blazin'; an' now an' then
    Thar come a rustle an' sort of rush,
A rattle a-sneakin' away from the blaze,
    Thro' the rattlin', cracklin' grey sage bush.

IV.

We'd chanc'd that night on a pootyish lot,
    Witn a tol'ble show of tall, sweet grass—
We was takin' Speredo's drove across
    The Rockies, by way of " Old Spookses' Pass "—
An' a mite of a creek went crinklin' down,
    Like a " pocket " bust in the rocks overhead,
Consid'able shrunk, by the summer drought,
    To a silver streak in its gravelly bed.

V.

'Twas a fairish spot fur to camp a' night;
    An' chipper I felt, tho' sort of skeer'd
That them two cowboys with only me,
    Couldn't boss three thousand head of a herd.
I took the fust of the watch myself;
    An' as the red sun down the mountains sprang,
I roll'd a fresh quid, an' got on the back
    Of my peart leetle chunk of a tough mustang.

VI.

An' Possum Billy was sleepin' sound,
  Es only a cowboy knows how to sleep;
An' Tommy's snores would hev made a old
  Buffalo bull feel kind o' cheap.
Wal, pard, I reckin' thar's no sech time
  For dwind'lin' a chap in his own conceit,
Es when them mountains an' awful stars,
  Jest hark to the tramp of his mustang's feet.

VII.

It 'pears to me that them solemn hills
  Beckin' them stars so big an' calm,
An' whisper, "Make tracks this way, my friends,
  We've ring'd in here a specimen man;
He's here alone, so we'll take a look
  Thro' his ganzy an' vest, an' his blood an' bone,
An post ourselves as to whether his heart
  Is *flesh*, or a rotten, made-up stone!"

VIII.

An' it's often seemed, on a midnight watch,
  When the mountains blacken'd the dry, brown sod,
That a chap, if he shut his eyes, might grip
  The great kind hand of his Father-God.
I rode round the herd at a sort of walk—
  The shadders come stealin' thick an' black;
I'd jest got to leave tew that thar chunk
  Of a mustang tew keep in the proper track.

IX.

Ever see'd a herd ring'd in at night?
    Wal, it's sort of cur'us,—the watchin' sky,
The howl of coyotes—a great black mass,
    With thar an' thar the gleam of a eye
An' the white of a horn—an', now an' then,
    An' old bull liftin' his shaggy head,
With a beller like a broke-up thunder growl—
    An' the summer lightnin', quick an' red,

X.

Twistin' an' turnin' amid the stars,
    Silent as snakes at play in the grass,
An' plungin' thar fangs in the bare old skulls
    Of the mountains, frownin' above the Pass.
An' all so still, that the leetle creek,
    Twinklin' an crinklin' from stone to stone,
Grows louder an' louder, an' fills the air
    With a cur'us sort of a singin' tone.
It ain't no matter wherever ye be,
    (I'll 'low it's a cur'us sort of case)
Whar thar's runnin' water, it's sure to speak
    Of folks tew home an' the old home place;

XI.

An' yer bound tew listen an' hear it talk,
    Es yer mustang crunches the dry, bald sod;
Fur I reckin' the hills, an' stars, an' creek
    Are all of 'em preachers sent by God.

An' them mountains talk tew a chap this way :
　"Climb, if ye can, ye degenerate cuss !"
An' the stars smile down on a man, an say,
　" Come higher, poor critter, come up tew us !"

XII.

An' I reckin', pard, thar is One above
　The highest old star that a chap can see,
An' He says, in a solid, etarnal way,
　" Ye never can stop till ye get to ME !"
Good fur Him, tew ! fur I calculate
　HE ain't the One to dodge an' tew shirk,
Or waste a mite of the things He's made,
　Or knock off till He's finished His great Day's work !

XIII.

We've got to labor an' strain an' snort
　Along thet road thet He's planned an' made ;
Don't matter a mite He's cut His line
　Tew run over a 'tarnal, tough up-grade ;
An' if some poor sinner ain't built tew hold
　Es big a head of steam es the next,
An' keeps slippin' an' slidin' 'way down hill,
　Why, He don't make out that He's awful vex'd.

XIV.

Fur He knows He made Him in that thar way,
　Somewhars tew fit in His own great plan ;
An' He ain't the Bein' tew pour His wrath
　On the head of thet slimpsy an' slippery man,

An' He says tew the feller, "Look here, my son,
    You're the worst hard case that ever I see,
But be thet it takes ye a million y'ars,
    Ye never can stop till ye git tew ME!"

XV.

Them's my idees es I pann'd them out;
    Don't take no stock in them creeds that say,
Thar's a chap with horns thet's took control
    Of the rollin' stock on thet up-grade way,
Thet's free to tote up es ugly a log
    Es grows in his big bush grim an' black,
An' slyly put it across the rails,
    Tew hist a poor critter clar off the track.

XVI.

An' when he's pooty well busted an' smash'd,
    The devil comes smilin' an' bowin' round,
Says tew the Maker, "Guess ye don't keer
    Tew trouble with stock thet ain't parfactly sound;
Lemme tote him away—best ye can do—
    Neglected, I guess, tew build him with care;
I'll hide him in hell—better thet folks
    Shouldn't see him laid up on the track for repair!"

XVII.

Don't take no stock in them creeds at all;
    Ain't one of them cur'us sort of moles
Thet think the Maker is bound to let
    The devil git up a "corner" in souls.

Ye think I've put up a biggish stake?
  Wal, I'll bet fur all I'm wuth, d'ye see?
He ain't wuth shucks thet won't dar tew lay
  All his pile on his own idee!

XVIII.

Ye bet yer boots I am safe tew win,
  Es the chap thet's able tew smilin' smack
The ace he's been hidin' up his sleeve
  Kerslap on top of a feller's jack!
Es I wus sayin', the night wus dark,
  The lightnin' skippin' from star to star;
Thar wa'n't no clouds but a thread of mist,
  No sound but the coyotes yell afar,

XIX.

An' the noise of the creek as it called tew me,
  " Pard, don't ye mind the mossy, green spot
Whar a creek stood still fur a drowzin' spell
  Right in the midst of the old home lot?
Whar, right at sundown on Sabba'day,
  Ye skinn'd yerself of yer meetin' clothes,
An dove, like a duck, whar the water clar
  Shone up like glass through the lily-blows?

XX.

" Yer soul wus white es yer skin them days,
  Yer eyes es clar es the creek at rest;
The wust idee in yer head thet time
  Wus robbin' a bluebird's swingin' nest.

Now ain't ye changed? declar fur it, pard ;
   Thet creek would question, it 'pears tew me,
Ef ye looked in its waters agin tew night,
   'Who may this old cuss of a sinner be?'"

XXI.

Thet wus the style thet thet thar creek
   In " Old Spookses' Pass," in the Rockies, talked ;
Drowzily list'nin' I rode round the herd,
   When all of a sudden the mustang balked,
An' shied with a snort ; I never know'd
   Thet tough leetle critter tew show a scare
In storm or dark ; but he jest scrouch'd down,
   With his nostrils snuffin' the damp, cool air,

XXII.

An' his flanks a-quiver. Shook up? Wal, yes
   Guess'd we hev heaps of tarnation fun ;
I calculated quicker'n light
   That the herd would be off on a healthy run.
But thar warn't a stir tew horn or hoof ;
   The herd, like a great black mist, lay spread,
While har an' thar a grazin' bull
   Loom'd up, like a mighty " thunder head."

XXIII.

I riz in my saddle an' star'd around—
   On the mustang's neck I felt the sweat ;
Thar wus nuthin' tew see—sort of felt the har
   Commencin' tew crawl on my scalp, ye bet !

Felt kind of cur'us—own up I did ;
 Felt sort of dry in my mouth an' throat.
Sez I, "Ye ain't goin' tew scare, old hoss,
 At a prowlin' cuss of a blamed coyote ?"

XXIV.

But 'twan't no coyote nor prowlin' beast,
 Nor rattle a-wrigglin' through the grass,
Nor a lurkin' red-skin— 'twan't my way
 In a game like that to sing out, " I pass !"
But I know'd when I glimps'd the rollin' whites,
 The sparks from the black of the mustang's eye,
Thar wus *somethin'* waltzin' up thet way
 Thet would send them critters off on the fly !

XXV.

In the night-air's tremblin', shakin' hands
 Felt it beatin' kerslap onto me,
Like them waves thet chas'd thet President chap
 Thet went on the war-trail in old Judee.
The air wus bustin'—but silent es death ;
 An' lookin' up, in a second I seed
The sort of sky thet allers looks down
 On the rush an' the roar of a night stampede.

XXVI.

Tearin' along the indigo sky
 Wus a drove of clouds, snarl'd an' black ;
Scuddin' along to'ards the risin' moon,
 Like the sweep of a darn'd hungry pack

Of preairie wolves to'ard a bufferler,
  The heft of the herd, left out of sight ;
I dror'd my breath right hard, fur I know'd
  We wus in fur a 'tarnal run thet night.

XXVII.

Quiet ?   Ye bet ! The mustang scrounch'd,
  His neck stretch'd out an' his nostrils wide ;
The moonshine swept, a white river down,
  The black of the mighty mountain's side,
Lappin' over an' over the stuns an' brush
  In whirls an' swirls of leapin' light,
Makin' straight fur the herd, whar black an' still,
  It stretch'd away to the left an' right

XXVIII.

On the level lot ;—I tell ye, pard,
  I know'd when it touch'd the first black hide,
Me an' the mustang would hev a show
  Fur a breezy bit of an' evenin' ride !
One ! it flow'd over a homely pine
  Thet riz from a cranny, lean an' lank,
A cleft of the mountain ;— reckinin' two,
  It slapp'd onto an' old steer's heavin' flank,

XXIX.

Es sound he slept on the skirt of the herd,
  Dreamin' his dreams of the sweet blue grass
On the plains below ; an' afore it touched
  The other wall of " Old Spookses' Pass "

The herd wus up!—not one at a time,
   Thet ain't the style in a midnight run,—
They wus up an' off like es all thair minds
   Wus roll'd in the hide of only one!

XXX.

I've fit in a battle, an' heerd the guns
   Blasphemin' God with their devils' yell;
Heerd the stuns of a fort like thunder crash
   In front of the scream of a red-hot shell;
But thet thar poundin' of iron hoofs,
   The clatter of horns, the peltin' sweep
Of three thousand head of a runnin' herd,
   Made all of them noises kind of cheap.

XXXI.

The Pass jest open'd its giant throat
   An' its lips of granite, an' let a roar
Of answerin' echoes; the mustang buck'd,
   Then answer'd the bridle; an', pard, afore
The twink of a fire-bug, lifted his legs
   Over stuns an' brush, like a lopin' deer—
A smart leetle critter! An' thar wus I
   'Longside of the plungin' leadin' steer!

XXXII.

A low-set critter, not much account
   For heft or looks, but one of them sort
Thet kin fetch a herd at his darn'd heels
   With a toss of his horns or a mite of a snort,

Fur a fight or a run; an' thar wus I,
  Pressin' clus to the steel of his heavin' flank,
An' cussin' an' shoutin'—while overhead
  The moon in the black clouds tremblin' sank,

XXXIII.

Like a bufferler overtook by the wolves
  An' pull'd tew the ground by the scuddin' pack.
The herd rush'd on with a din an' crash,
  Dim es a shadder, vast an' black;
Couldn't tell ef a hide wus black or white,
  But from the dim surges a-roarin' by
Bust long red flashes—the flamin' light
  From some old steer's furious an' scareful eye.

XXXIV.

Thet pass in the Rockies fairly roar'd;
  An sudden' es winkin' came the bang
An rattle of thunder. Tew see the grit
  Of thet peart little chunk of a tough mustang!
Not a buck nor a shy!—he gev a snort
  Thet shook the foam on his steamin' hide,
An' leap'd along.—Wal, pard, ye bet
  I'd a healthy show fur a lively ride.

XXXV.

An' them cowboys slept in the leetle camp,
  Calm es ~~three~~ kids in a truckle bed;
Declar the crash wus enough tew put
  Life in the dust of the sleepin' dead!

The thunder kept droppin' its awful shells,
   One at a minute, on mountain an' rock :
The pass with its stone lips thunder'd back ;
   An' the rush an' roar an' whirlin' shock
Of the runnin' herd wus fit tew bust
   A tenderfoot's heart hed he chanc'd along ;
But I jest let out of my lungs an' throat
   A rippin' old verse of a herdsman's song,

XXXVI.

An' sidl'd the mustang closer up,
   'Longside of the leader, an' hit him flat
On his steamin' flank with a lightsome stroke
   Of the end of my limber lariat ;
He never swerv'd, an' we thunder'd on,
   Black in the blackness, red in the red
Of the lightnin' blazin' with ev'ry clap
   That bust from the black guns overhead !

XXXVII.

The mustang wus shod, an' the lightnin' bit
   At his iron shoes each step he run,
Then plung'd in the yearth—we rode in flame,
   Fur the flashes roll'd inter only one,
Same es the bellers made one big roar ;
   Yet thro' the whirl of din an' flame
I sung an' shouted, an' call'd the steer
   I sidl'd agin by his own front name,

XXXVIII.

An' struck his side with my fist an' foot—
　'Twas jest like hittin' a rushin' stone,
An' he thunder'd ahead—I couldn't boss
　The critter a mossel, I'm free tew own.
The sweat come a-pourin' down my beard;
　Ef ye wonder wharfor, jest ye spread
Yerself fur a ride with a runnin' herd,
　A yawnin' gulch half a mile ahead.

XXXIX.

Three hundred foot from its grinnin' lips
　Tew the roarin' stream on its stones below.
Once more I hurl'd the mustang up
　Agin the side of the cuss call'd Joe;
'Twan't a mite of use—he riz his heels
　Up in the air, like a scuddin' colt;
The herd mass'd closer, an' hurl'd down
　The roarin' Pass, like a thunderbolt.

XL.

I couldn't rein off—seem'd swept along
　In the rush an' roar an' thunderin' crash;
The lightnin' struck at the runnin' herd
　With a crack like the stroke of a cowboy's lash.
Thar! I could see it; I tell ye, pard,
　Things seem'd whittl'd down sort of fine—
We wusn't five hundred feet from the gulch,
　With its mean little fringe of scrubby pine.

XLI.

What could stop us? I grit my teeth ;
　　Think I pray'd—ain't sartin of thet ;
When, whizzin' an' singin', thar came the rush
　　Right past my face of a lariat !
" Bully fur you, old pard ! " I roar'd,
　　Es it whizz'd roun' the leader's steamin' chest,
An' I wheel'd the mustang fur all he was wuth
　　Kerslap on the side of the old steer's breast.

XLII.

He gev a snort, an' I see him swerve—
　　I foller'd his shoulder clus an' tight ;
Another swerve, an' the herd begun
　　To swing around.—Shouts I, " All right
" Ye've fetch'd 'em now !" The mustang gave
　　A small, leettle whinney. I felt him flinch.
Sez I, " Ye ain't goin' tew weaken now,
　　Old feller, an' me in this darn'd pinch ?"

XLIII.

" No," sez he, with his small, prickin' ears,
　　Plain es a human could speak ; an' me—
I turn'd my head tew glimpse ef I could,
　　Who might the chap with the lariat be.
Wal, Pard, I weaken'd—ye bet yer life !
　　Thar wasn't a human in sight around,
But right in front of me come the beat
　　Of a hoss's hoofs on the tremblin' ground—

XLIV.

Steddy an' heavy—a slingin' lope ;
  A hefty critter with biggish bones
Might make jest sich—could hear the hoofs
  Es they struck on the rattlin', rollin' stones—
The jingle of bit—an' clar an' shrill
  A whistle es ever left cowboy's lip,
An' cuttin' the air, the long, fine hiss
  Of the whirlin' lash of a cowboy's whip.

XLV.

I crowded the mustang back, ontil
  He riz on his haunches—an' I sed,
"In the Maker's name, who may ye be?"
  Sez a vice, "Old feller, jest ride ahead!"
"All right!" sez I, an' I shook the rein.
  "Ye've turn'd the herd in a hansum style—
Whoever ye be, I'll not back down!"
  An' I didn't, neither,—ye bet yer pile!

XLVI.

Clus on the heels of that unseen hoss,
  I rode on the side of the turnin' herd,
An' once in a while I answer'd back
  A shout or a whistle or cheerin' word—
From lips no lightnin' was strong tew show.
  'Twas sort of scareful, that midnight ride ;
But we'd got our backs tew the gulch—fur that
  I'd hev foller'd a curiouser sort of guide !

XLVII.

'Twas kind of scareful tew watch the herd,
　Es the plungin' leaders squirm'd an' shrank—
Es I heerd the flick of the unseen lash
　Hiss on the side of a steamin' flank.
Guess the feller was smart at the work !
　We work'd them leaders round, ontil
They overtook the tail of the herd,
　An' the hull of the crowd begun tew " mill."

XLVIII.

Round spun the herd in a great black wheel,
　Slower an' slower—ye've seen beneath
A biggish torrent a whirlpool spin,
　Its waters black es the face of Death ?
'Pear'd sort of like that the " millin'" herd
　We kept by the leaders—HIM and me,
Neck by neck, an' he sung a tune,
　About a young gal, nam'd Betsey Lee !

XLIX.

Jine in the chorus ?　Wal, yas, I did.
　He sung like a regilar mockin' bird.
An' us cowboys allus sing out ef tew calm
　The scare, ef we can, of a runnin' herd.
Slower an' slower wheel'd round the " mill" ;
　The maddest old steer of a leader slow'd ;
Slower an' slower sounded the hoofs
　Of the hoss that HIM in front of me rode.

L.

Fainter an' fainter grow'd that thar song
    Of Betsey Lee an' her har of gold ;
Fainter an' fainter grew the sound
    Of the unseen hoofs on the tore-up mold.
The leadin' steer, that cuss of a Joe
    Stopp'd an' shook off the foam an' the sweat,
With a stamp and a beller—the run was done,
    Wus glad of it, tew, yer free tew bet !

LI.

The herd slow'd up—an' stood in a mass
    Of blackness, lit by the lightnin's eye ;
An' the mustang cower'd es *something* swept
    Clus to his wet flank in passin' by.
"Good night tew ye, Pard !" "Good night," sez I,
    Strainin' my sight on the empty air ;
The har riz rustlin' up on my head,
    Now that I hed time tew scare.

LII.

The mustang flinch'd till his saddle girth
    Scrap'd on the dust of the tremblin' ground—
There cum a laugh—the crack of a whip,
    A whine like the cry of a well pleas'd hound,
The noise of a hoss thet rear'd an' sprang
    At the touch of a spur—then all was still ;
But the sound of the thunder dyin' down
    On the stony breast of the nighest hill !

LIII.

The herd went back to its rest an' feed,
    Es quiet a crowd es ever wore hide;
An' them boys in camp never heerd a lisp
    Of the thunder an' crash of that run an' ride.
An' I'll never forget, while a wild cat claws,
    Or a cow loves a nibble of sweet blue grass,
The cur'us pardner that rode with me
    In the night stampede in "Old Spookses Pass!"

THE HELOT.

I.

Low the sun beat on the land,
    Red on vine and plain and wood ;
With the wine-cup in his hand,
    Vast the Helot herdsman stood.

II.

Quench'd the fierce Achean gaze,
    Dorian foemen paus'd before,
Where cold Sparta snatch'd her bays
    At Achaea's stubborn door.

III.

Still with thews of iron bound,
    Vastly the Achean rose,
Godward from the brazen ground,
    High before his Spartan foes.

IV.

Still the strength his fathers knew
   (Dauntless when the foe they fac'd)
Vein and muscle bounded through,
   Tense his Helot sinews brac'd.

V.

Still the constant womb of Earth,
   Blindly moulded all her part :
As, when to a lordly birth,
   Achean freemen left her heart.

VI.

Still, insensate mother, bore
   Goodly sons for Helot graves ;
Iron necks that meekly wore
   Sparta's yoke as Sparta's slaves.

VII.

Still, O God mock'd mother ! she
   Smil'd upon her sons of clay :
Nurs'd them on her breast and knee,
   Shameless in the shameful day.

VIII.

Knew not old Achea's fires
   Burnt no more in souls or veins—
Godlike hosts of high desires
   Died to clank of Spartan chains.

IX.

Low the sun beat on the land,
    Purple slope and olive wood;
With the wine cup in his hand,
    Vast the Helot herdsman stood.

X.

As long, gnarl'd roots enclasp
    Some red boulder, fierce entwine
His strong fingers, in their grasp
    Bowl of bright Caecuban wine.

XI.

From far Marsh of Amyclae,
    Sentried by lank poplars tall—
Thro' the red slant of the day,
    Shrill pipes did lament and call.

XII.

Pierc'd the swaying air sharp pines,
    Thyrsi-like, the gilded ground
Clasp'd black shadows of brown vines,
    Swallows beat their mystic round.

XIII.

Day was at her high unrest;
    Fever'd with the wine of light,
Loosing all her golden vest,
    Reel'd she towards the coming night.

XIV.

Fierce and full her pulses beat;
　　Bacchic throbs the dry earth shook;
Stirr'd the hot air wild and sweet;
　　Madden'd ev'ry vine-dark brook.

XV.

Had a red grape never burst,
　　All its heart of fire out;
To the red vat all athirst,
　　To the treader's song and shout:

XVI.

Had the red grape died a grape;
　　Nor, sleek daughter of the vine,
Found her unknown soul take shape
　　In the wild flow of the wine:

XVII.

Still had reel'd the yellow haze:
　　Still had puls'd the sun pierc'd sod:
Still had throbb'd the vine clad days:
　　To the pulses of their God.

XVIII.

Fierce the dry lips of the earth
　　Quaff'd the subtle Bacchic soul:
Felt its rage and felt its mirth,
　　Wreath'd as for the banquet bowl.

XIX.

Sapphire-breasted Bacchic priest
    Stood the sky above the lands;
Sun and Moon at East and West,
    Brazen cymbals in his hands.

XX.

Temples, altars, smote no more,
    Sharply white as brows of Gods:
From the long, sleek, yellow shore,
    Oliv'd hill or dusky sod,

XXI.

Gaz'd the anger'd Gods, while he,
    Bacchus, made their temples his;
Flush'd their marble silently
    With the red light of his kiss.

XXII.

Red the arches of his feet
    Spann'd grape-gleaming vales; the earth
Reel'd from grove to marble street,
    Mad with echoes of his mirth.

XXIII.

Nostrils widen'd to the air,
    As above the wine brimm'd bowl:
Men and women everywhere
    Breath'd the fierce, sweet Bacchic soul.

XXIV.

Flow'd the vat and roar'd the beam,
  Laugh'd the must; while far and shrill,
Sweet as notes in Pan-born dream,
  Loud pipes sang by vale and hill.

XXV.

Earth was full of mad unrest,
  While red Bacchus held his state;
And her brown vine-girdl'd breast
  Shook to his wild joy and hate.

XXVI.

Strife crouch'd red ey'd in the vine;
  In its tendrils Eros strayed;
Anger rode upon the wine;
  ·Laughter on the cup-lip play'd.

XXVII.

Day was at her chief unrest—
  Red the light on plain and wood:
Slavish ey'd and still of breast,
  Vast the Helot herdsman stood:

XXVIII.

Wide his hairy nostrils blew,
  Maddning incense breathing up;
Oak to iron sinews grew,
  Round the rich Caecuban cup.

XXIX.

" Drink, dull slave !" the Spartan said,
    " Drink, until the Helot clod
" Feel within him subtly bred
    " Kinship to the drunken God !

XXX.

" Drink, until the leaden blood
    " Stirs and beats about thy brain :
" Till the hot Caecuban flood
    " Drown the iron of thy chain.

XXXI.

" Drink, till even madness flies
    " At the nimble wine's pursuit ;
" Till the God within thee lies
    " Trampled by the earth-born brute.

XXXII.

" Helot drink—nor spare the wine ;
    " Drain the deep, the madd'ning bowl,
" Flesh and sinews, slave, are mine,
    " Now I claim thy Helot soul.

XXXIII.

" Gods ! ye love our Sparta ; ye
    " Gave with vine that leaps and runs
" O'er her slopes, these slaves to be
    " Mocks and warnings to her sons !

XXXIV.

" Thou, my Hermos, turn thy eyes,
　" (God-touch'd still their frank, bold blue)
" On the Helot—mark the rise
　" Of the Bacchic riot through

XXXV.

" Knotted vein, and surging breast:
　" Mark the wild, insensate mirth :
" God-ward boast—the driv'ling jest,
　" Till he grovel to the earth.

XXXVI.

" Drink, dull slave," the Spartan cried :
　Meek the Helot touch'd the brim ;
Scented all the purple tide :
　Drew the Bacchic soul to him.

XXXVII.

Cold the thin lipp'd Spartan smiled :
　Couch'd beneath the weighted vine,
Large-ey'd, gaz'd the Spartan child,
　On the Helot and the wine.

XXXIX.

Rose pale Doric shafts behind,
　Stern and strong, and thro' and thro',
Weaving with the grape-breath'd wind,
　Restless swallows call'd and flew.

XXXIX.

Dropp'd the rose-flush'd doves and hung,
    On the fountains murmuring brims;
To the bronz'd vine Hermos clung—
    Silver-like his naked limbs

XL.

Flash'd and flush'd : rich copper'd leaves,
    Whiten'd by his ruddy hair;
Pallid as the marble eaves,
    Aw'd he met the Helot's stare.

XLI.

Clang'd the brazen goblet down;
    Marble-bred loud echoes stirr'd:
With fix'd fingers, knotted, brown,
    Dumb, the Helot grasp'd his beard.

XLII.

Heard the far pipes mad and sweet,
    All the ruddy hazes thrill:
Heard the loud beam crash and beat,
    In the red vat on the hill.

XLIII.

Wide his nostrils as a stag's
    Drew the hot wind's fiery bliss;
Red his lips as river flags,
    From the strong, Caecuban kiss.

XLIV.

On his swarthy temples grew,
    Purple veins like cluster'd grapes;
Past his rolling pupils blew,
    Wine-born, fierce, lascivious shapes.

XLV.

Cold the haughty Spartan smiled—
    His the power to knit that day,
Bacchic fires, insensate, wild,
    To the grand Achean clay.

XLVI.

His the might—hence his the right!
    Who should bid him pause? nor Fate
Warning pass'd before his sight,
    Dark-robed and articulate.

XLVII.

No black omens on his eyes,
    Sinistre—God-sent, darkly broke;
Nor from ruddy earth nor skies,
    Portends to him mutely spoke.

XLVIII.

" Lo," he said, " he maddens now!
    " Flames divine do scathe the clod:
" Round his reeling Helot brow
    " Stings the garland of the God."

XLIX.

" Mark, my Hermos—turn to steel
    The soft tendons of thy soul !
Watch the God beneath the heel
    Of the strong brute swooning roll !

L.

" Shame, my Hermos ! honey-dew
    Breeds not on the Spartan spear ;
Steel thy mother-eyes of blue,
    Blush to death that weakling tear.

LI.

" Nay, behold ! breed Spartan scorn
    Of the red lust of the wine ;
Watch the God himself down-borne
    By the brutish rush of swine !

LII.

" Lo, the magic of the drink !
    At the nimble wine's pursuit,
See the man-half 'd satyr sink
    All the human in the brute !

LIII.

" Lo, the magic of the cup !
    Watch the frothing Helot rave !
As great buildings labour up
    From the corpse of slaughter'd slave,

LIV.

" Build the Spartan virtue high
    From the Helot's wine-dead soul;
Scorn the wild, hot flames that fly
    From the purple-hearted bowl!

LV.

" Helot clay! Gods! what its worth,
    Balanc'd with proud Sparta's rock?
Ours—its force to till the earth;
    Ours—its soul to gyve and mock!

LVI.

" Ours, its sullen might. Ye Gods!
    Vastly build the Achean clay;
Iron-breast our slavish clods—
    Ours their Helot souls to slay!

LVII.

" Knit great thews—smite sinews vast
    Into steel—build Helot bones
Iron-marrowed:—such will last
    Ground by ruthless Sparta's stones.

LVIII.

" Crown the strong brute satyr-wise!
    Narrow-wall his Helot brain;
Dash the soul from breast and eyes,
    Lash him toward the earth again.

LIX.

"Make a giant for our need,
  Weak to feel and strong to toil;
Dully-wise to dig or bleed
  On proud Sparta's alien soil!

LX.

"Gods! recall thy spark at birth,
  Lit his soul with high desire;
Blend him, grind him with the earth,
  Tread out old Achea's fire!

LXI.

"Lo, my Hermos! laugh and mark,
  See the swift mock of the wine;
Faints the primal, God-born spark,
  Trodden by the rush of swine!

LXII.

"Gods! ye love our Sparta—ye
  Gave with vine that leaps and runs
O'er her slopes, these slaves to be
  Mocks and warnings to her sons!"

LXIII.

Cold the haughty Spartan smil'd.
  Madd'ning from the purple hills
Sang the far pipes, sweet and wild.
  Red as sun-pierc'd daffodils

LXIV.

Neck-curv'd, serpent, silent, scaled
  With lock'd rainbows, stole the sea ;
On the sleek, long beaches ; wail'd
  Doves from column and from tree.

LXV.

Reel'd the mote swarm'd haze, and thick
  Beat the hot pulse of the air ;
In the Helot, fierce and quick,
  All his soul sprang from its lair.

LXVI.

As the drowzing tiger, deep
  In the dim cell, hears the shout
From the arena—from his sleep
  Launches to its thunders out—

LXVII.

So to fierce calls of the wine
  (Strong the red Caecuban bowl !)
From its slumber, deep, supine,
  Panted up the Helot soul.

LXVIII.

At his blood-flush'd eye-balls rear'd,
  (Mad and sweet came pipes and songs),
Rous'd at last the wild soul glar'd,
  Spear-thrust with a million wrongs.

LXIX.

Past—the primal, senseless bliss;
   Past—red laughter of the grapes;
Past—the wine's first honey'd kiss;
   Past—the wine-born, wanton shapes!

LXX.

Still the Helot stands—his feet
   Set like oak-roots; in his gaze
Black clouds roll and lightnings meet—
   Flames from old Achean days.

LXXI.

Who may quench the God-born fire,
   Pulsing at the soul's deep root?
Tyrants! grind it in the mire,
   Lo, it vivifies the brute!

LXXII.

Stings the chain-embruted clay,
   Senseless to his yoke-bound shame;
Goads him on to rend and slay,
   Knowing not the spurring flame.

LXXIII.

Tyrants, changeless stand the Gods!
   Nor their calm might yielded ye!
Not beneath thy chains and rods
   Dies man's God-gift, Liberty!

LXXIV.

Bruteward lash thy Helots—hold
    Brain and soul and clay in gyves;
Coin their blood and sweat in gold,
    Build thy cities on their lives.

LXXV.

Comes a day the spark divine
    Answers to the Gods who gave;
Fierce the hot flames pant and shine
    In the bruis'd breast of the slave!

LXXVI.

Changeless stand the Gods!—nor he
    Knows he answers their behest;
Feels the might of their decree
    In the blind rage of his breast.

LXXVII.

Tyrants! tremble when ye tread
    Down the servile Helot clods;
Under despot heel is bred
    The white anger of the Gods!

LXXVIII.

Thro' the shackle-canker'd dust,
    Thro' the gyv'd soul, foul and dark,
Force they, changeless Gods and just!
    Up the bright, eternal spark.

LXXIX.

Till, like lightnings vast and fierce,
   On the land its terror smites ;
Till its flames the tyrants pierce,
   Till the dust the despot bites !

LXXX.

Day was at its chief unrest,
   Stone from stone the Helot rose ;
Fix'd his eyes—his naked breast
   Iron-wall'd his inner throes.

LXXXI.

Rose-white in the dusky leaves,
   Shone the frank-ey'd Spartan child ;
Low the pale doves on the eaves,
   Made their soft moan, sweet and wild.

LXXXII.

Wand'ring winds, fire-throated, stole,
   Sybils whisp'ring from their books ;
With the rush of wine from bowl,
   Leap'd the tendril-darken'd brooks.

LXXXIII.

As the leathern cestus binds
   Tense the boxer's knotted hands ;
So the strong wine round him winds,
   Binds his thews to iron bands.

LXXXIV.

Changeless are the Gods—and bred
    All their wrath divine in him !
Bull-like fell his furious head,
    Swell'd vast cords on breast and limb.

LXXXV.

As loud-flaming stones are hurl'd
    From foul craters—thus the gods
Cast their just wrath on the world,
    From the mire of Helot clods.

LXXXVI.

Still the furious Helot stood,
    Staring thro' the shafted space ;
Dry-lipp'd for the Spartan blood,
    He of scourg'd Achea's race.

LXXXVII.

Sprang the Helot—roar'd the vine,
    Rent from grey, long-wedded stones—
From pale shaft and dusky pine,
    Beat the fury of his groans.

LXXXVIII.

Thunders inarticulate :
    Wordless curses, deep and wild ;
Reach'd the long pois'd sword of Fate,
    To the Spartan thro' his child.

LXXXIX.

On his knotted hands, upflung
    O'er his low'r'd front—all white,
Fair young Hermos quiv'ring hung;
    As the discus flashes bright

XC.

In the player's hand—the boy,
    Naked—blossom-pallid lay;
Rous'd to lust of bloody joy,
    Throbb'd the slave's embruted clay.

XCI.

Loud he laugh'd—the father sprang
    From the Spartan's iron mail!
Late—the bubbling death-cry rang
    On the hot pulse of the gale!

XCII.

As the shining discus flies,
    From the thrower's strong hand whirl'd;
Hermos cleft the air—his cries
    Lance-like to the Spartan hurl'd.

XCIII.

As the discus smites the ground,
    Smote his golden head the stone;
Of a tall shaft—burst a sound
    And but one—his dying groan!

XCIV.

Lo ! the tyrant's iron might !
    Lo ! the Helot's yokes and chains !
Slave-slain in the throbbing light
    Lay the sole child of his veins.

XCV.

Laugh'd the Helot loud and full,
    Gazing at his tyrant's face ;
Low'r'd his front like captive bull,
    Bellowing from the fields of Thrace.

XCVI.

Rose the pale shaft redly flush'd,
    Red with Bacchic light and blood ;
On its stone the Helot rush'd—
    Stone the tyrant Spartan stood.

XCVII.

Lo ! the magic of the wine
    From far marsh of Amyclae !
Bier'd upon the ruddy vine,
    Spartan dust and Helot lay !

XCVIII.

Spouse of Bacchus reel'd the day,
    Red track'd on the throbbing sods ;
Dead—but free—the Helot lay,
    Just and changeless stand the Gods !

MALCOLM'S KATIE: A LOVE STORY.

Part I.

Max plac'd a ring on little Katie's hand,
A silver ring that he had beaten out
From that same sacred coin— first well-priz'd wage
For boyish labour, kept thro' many years.
"See, Kate," he said, "I had no skill to shape
Two hearts fast bound together, so I grav'd
Just K. and M., for Katie and for Max."
"But, look; you've run the lines in such a way,
That M. is part of K., and K. of M.,"
Said Katie, smiling. "Did you mean it thus?
I like it better than the double hearts."
"Well, well," he said, "but womankind is wise!
Yet tell me, dear, will such a prophecy
Not hurt you sometimes, when I am away?
Will you not seek, keen ey'd, for some small break
In those deep lines, to part the K. and M.
For you? Nay, Kate, look down amid the globes
Of those large lilies that our light canoe
Divides, and see within the polish'd pool

That small, rose face of yours,—so dear, so fair,—
A seed of love to cleave into a rock,
And bourgeon thence until the granite splits
Before its subtle strength. I being gone—
Poor soldier of the axe—to bloodless fields,
(Inglorious battles, whether lost or won).
That sixteen summer'd heart of yours may say :
" ' I but was budding, and I did not know
My core was crimson and my perfume sweet ;
I did not know how choice a thing I am ;
I had not seen the sun, and blind I sway'd
To a strong wind, and thought because I sway'd,
'Twas to the wooer of the perfect rose—
That strong, wild wind has swept beyond my ken—
The breeze I love sighs thro' my ruddy leaves.' "
" O, words !" said Katie, blushing, " only words !
You build them up that I may push them down ;
If hearts are flow'rs, I know that flow'rs can root—
Bud, blossom, die—all in the same lov'd soil ;
They do so in my garden. I have made
Your heart my garden. If I am a bud
And only feel unfoldment—feebly stir
Within my leaves ; wait patiently ; some June,
I'll blush a full-blown rose, and queen it, dear,
In your lov'd garden. Tho' I be a bud,
My roots strike deep, and torn from that dear soil
Would shriek like mandrakes—those witch things I read
Of in your quaint old books. Are you content ?"
" Yes—crescent-wise—but not to round, full moon.
Look at yon hill that rounds so gently up
From the wide lake ; a lover king it looks,

In cloth of gold, gone from his bride and queen;
And yet delay'd, because her silver locks
Catch in his gilded fringes; his shoulders sweep
Into blue distance, and his gracious crest,
Not held too high, is plum'd with maple groves;—
One of your father's farms. A mighty man,
Self-hewn from rock, remaining rock through all."
" He loves me, Max," said Katie : " Yes, I know—
A rock is cup to many a crystal spring.
Well, he is rich; those misty, peak-roof'd barns—
Leviathans rising from red seas of grain—
Are full of ingots, shaped like grains of wheat.
His flocks have golden fleeces, and his herds
Have monarchs worshipful, as was the calf
Aaron call'd from the furnace; and his ploughs,
Like Genii chained, snort o'er his mighty fields.
He has a voice in Council and in Church—"
" He work'd for all," said Katie, somewhat pain'd.
" Aye, so, dear love, he did; I heard him tell
How the first field upon his farm was plough'd.
He and his brother Reuben, stalwart lads,
Yok'd themselves, side by side, to the new plough;
Their weaker father, in the grey of life
(But rather the wan age of poverty
Than many winters), in large, gnarl'd hands
The plunging handles held; with mighty strains
They drew the ripping beak through knotted sod,
Thro' tortuous lanes of blacken'd, smoking stumps;
And past great flaming brush heaps, sending out
Fierce summers, beating on their swollen brows.
O, such a battle! had we heard of serfs

A LOVE STORY.

Driven to like hot conflict with the soil,
Armies had march'd and navies swiftly sail'd
To burst their gyves. But here's the little point—
The polish'd di'mond pivot on which spins
The wheel of Difference—they OWN'D the rugged soil,
And fought for love—dear love of wealth and pow'r,
And honest ease and fair esteem of men ;
One's blood heats at it !" "Yet you said such fields
Were all inglorious," Katie, wondering, said.
" Inglorious ? yes ; they make no promises
Of Star or Garter, or the thundering guns
That tell the earth her warriors are dead.
Inglorious ! aye, the battle done and won
Means not—a throne propp'd up with bleaching bones ;
A country sav'd with smoking seas of blood ;
A flag torn from the foe with wounds and death ;
Or Commerce, with her housewife foot upon
Colossal bridge of slaughter'd savages,
The Cross laid on her brawny shoulder, and
In one sly, mighty hand her reeking sword ;
And in the other all the woven cheats
From her dishonest looms. Nay, none of these.
It means—four walls, perhaps a lowly roof ;
Kine in a peaceful posture ; modest fields ;
A man and woman standing hand in hand
In hale old age, who, looking o'er the land,
Say : ' Thank the Lord, it all is mine and thine !'
It means, to such thew'd warriors of the Axe
As your own father ;—well, it means, sweet Kate,
Outspreading circles of increasing gold,
A name of weight ; one little daughter heir.

Who must not wed the owner of an axe,
Who owns naught else but some dim, dusky woods
In a far land ; two arms indifferent strong—"
"And Katie's heart," said Katie, with a smile ;
For yet she stood on that smooth, violet plain,
Where nothing shades the sun ; nor quite believed
Those blue peaks closing in were aught but mist
Which the gay sun could scatter with a glance.
For Max, he late had touch'd their stones, but yet
He saw them seam'd with gold and precious ores,
Rich with hill flow'rs and musical with rills.
" Or that same bud that will be Katies heart,
Against the time your deep, dim woods are clear'd,
And I have wrought my father to relent."
" How will you move him, sweet ? why, he will rage
And fume and anger, striding o'er his fields,
Until the last bought king of herds lets down
His lordly front, and rumbling thunder from
His polish'd chest, returns his chiding tones.
How will you move him, Katie, tell me how ?"
" I'll kiss him and keep still —that way is sure,"
Said Katie, smiling. " I have often tried."
"God speed the kiss," said Max, and Katie sigh'd,
With pray'rful palms close seal'd, " God speed the axe !"

O, light canoe, where dost thou glide ?
Below thee gleams no silver'd tide,
But concave heaven's chiefest pride.

Above thee burns Eve's rosy bar;
Below thee throbs her darling star;
Deep 'neath thy keel her round worlds are!

———

Above, below, O sweet surprise,
To gladden happy lover's eyes;
No earth, no wave—all jewell'd skies!

———

PART II.

The South Wind laid his moccasins aside,
Broke his gay calumet of flow'rs, and cast
His useless wampun, beaded with cool dews,
Far from him, northward; his long, ruddy spear
Flung sunward, whence it came, and his soft locks
Of warm, fine haze grew silver as the birch.
His wigwam of green leaves began to shake;
The crackling rice-beds scolded harsh like squaws;
The small ponds pouted up their silver lips;
The great lakes ey'd the mountains, whisper'd "Ugh!"
"Are ye so tall, O chiefs? Not taller than
Our plumes can reach." And rose a little way,
As panthers stretch to try their velvet limbs,
And then retreat to purr and bide their time.
At morn the sharp breath of the night arose
From the wide prairies, in deep-struggling seas,

In rolling breakers, bursting to the sky;
In tumbling surfs, all yellow'd faintly thro'
With the low sun—in mad, conflicting crests,
Voic'd with low thunder from the hairy throats
Of the mist-buried herds; and for a man
To stand amid the cloudy roll and moil,
The phantom waters breaking overhead,
Shades of vex'd billows bursting on his breast,
Torn caves of mist wall'd with a sudden gold,
Reseal'd as swift as seen—broad, shaggy fronts,
Fire-ey'd and tossing on impatient horns
The wave impalpable—was but to think
A dream of phantoms held him as he stood.
The late, last thunders of the summer crash'd,
Where shrieked great eagles, lords of naked cliffs.
The pulseless forest, lock'd and interlock'd
So closely, bough with bough, and leaf with leaf,
So serf'd by its own wealth, that while from high
The moons of summer kiss'd its green-gloss'd locks;
And round its knees the merry West Wind danc'd;
And round its ring, compacted emerald;
The south wind crept on moccasins of flame;
And the red fingers of th' impatient sun
Pluck'd at its outmost fringes—its dim veins
Beat with no life—its deep and dusky heart,
In a deep trance of shadow, felt no throb
To such soft wooing answer: thro' its dream
Brown rivers of deep waters sunless stole;
Small creeks sprang from its mosses, and amaz'd,
Like children in a wigwam curtain'd close
Above the great, dead heart of some red chief,

Slipp'd on soft feet, swift stealing through the gloom,
Eager for light and for the frolic winds.
In this shrill moon the scouts of winter ran
From the ice-belted north, and whistling shafts
Struck maple and struck sumach—and a blaze
Ran swift from leaf to leaf, from bough to bough ;
Till round the forest flash'd a belt of flame
And inward lick'd its tongues of red and gold
To the deep, tranied inmost heart of all.
Rous'd the still heart—but all too late, too late.
Too late, the branches welded fast with leaves,
Toss'd, loosen'd, to the winds—too late the sun
Pour'd his last vigor to the deep, dark cells
Of the dim wood. The keen, two-bladed Moon
Of Falling Leaves roll'd up on crested mists
And where the lush, rank boughs had foiled the sun
In his red prime, her pale, sharp fingers crept
After the wind and felt about the moss,
And seem'd to pluck from shrinking twig and stem
The burning leaves—while groan'd the shudd'ring wood.
Who journey'd where the prairies made a pause,
Saw burnish'd ramparts flaming in the sun,
With beacon fires, tall on their rustling walls.
And when the vast, horn'd herds at sunset drew
Their sullen masses into one black cloud,
Rolling thund'rous o'er the quick pulsating plain,
They seem'd to sweep between two fierce red suns
Which, hunter-wise, shot at their glaring balls
Keen shafts, with scarlet feathers and gold barbs,
By round, small lakes with thinner forests fring'd,
More jocund woods that sung about the feet

And crept along the shoulders of great cliffs ;
The warrior stags, with does and tripping fawns,
Like shadows black upon the throbbing mist
Of Evening's rose, flash'd thro' the singing woods—
Nor tim'rous, sniff'd the spicy, cone-breath'd air ;
For never had the patriarch of the herd
Seen limn'd against the farthest rim of light
Of the low-dipping sky, the plume or bow
Of the red hunter ; nor when stoop'd to drink,
Had from the rustling rice-beds heard the shaft
Of the still hunter hidden in its spears ;
His bark canoe close-knotted in its bronze,
His form as stirless as the brooding air,
His dusky eyes, too, fix'd, unwinking, fires ;
His bow-string tighten'd till it subtly sang
To the long throbs, and leaping pulse that roll'd
And beat within his knotted, naked breast.
There came a morn. The Moon of Falling Leaves,
With her twin silver blades had only hung
Above the low set cedars of the swamp
For one brief quarter, when the sun arose
Lusty with light and full of summer heat,
And pointing with his arrows at the blue,
Clos'd, wigwam curtains of the sleeping moon,
Laugh'd with the noise of arching cataracts,
And with the dove-like cooing of the woods,
And with the shrill cry of the diving loon
And with the wash of saltless, rounded seas,
And mock'd the white moon of the Falling Leaves.
" Esa ! esa ! shame upon you, Pale Face !
" Shame upon you, moon of evil witches !

"Have you kill'd the happy, laughing Summer?
"Have you slain the mother of the Flowers
"With your icy spells of might and magic?
"Have you laid her dead within my arms?
"Wrapp'd her, mocking, in a rainbow blanket,
"Drown'd her in the frost mist of your anger?
"She is gone a little way before me;
"Gone an arrow's flight beyond my vision;
"She will turn again and come to meet me,
"With the ghosts of all the slain flowers,
"In a blue mist round her shining tresses;
"In a blue smoke in her naked forests—
"She will linger, kissing all the branches,
"She will linger, touching all the places,
"Bare and naked, with her golden fingers,
"Saying, 'Sleep, and dream of me, my children;
"'Dream of me, the mystic Indian Summer;
"'I, who, slain by the cold Moon of Terror,
"'Can return across the path of Spirits,
"'Bearing still my heart of love and fire;
"'Looking with my eyes of warmth and splendour;
"'Whisp'ring lowly thro' your sleep of sunshine.
"'I, the laughing Summer, am not turn'd
"'Into dry dust, whirling on the prairies,—
"'Into red clay, crush'd beneath the snowdrifts.
"'I am still the mother of sweet flowers
"'Growing but an arrow's flight beyond you—
"'In the Happy Hunting Ground—the quiver
"'Of great Manitou, where all the arrows
"'He has shot from his great bow of Pow'r,
"'With its clear, bright, singing cord of Wisdom,

" ' Are re-gather'd, plum'd again and brighten'd,
" ' And shot out, re-barb'd with Love and Wisdom ;
" ' Always shot, and evermore returning.
" ' Sleep, my children, smiling in your heart-seeds
" ' At the spirit words of Indian Summer !' "
" Thus, O Moon of Falling Leaves, I mock you !
" Have you slain my gold-ey'd squaw, the Summer ?"
The mighty morn strode laughing up the land,
And Max, the labourer and the lover, stood
Within the forest's edge, beside a tree ;
The mossy king of all the woody tribes,
Whose clatt'ring branches rattl'd, shuddering,
As the bright axe cleav'd moon-like thro' the air,
Waking strange thunders, rousing echoes link'd
From the full, lion-throated roar, to sighs
Stealing on dove-wings thro' the distant aisles.
Swift fell the axe, swift follow'd roar on roar,
Till the bare woodland bellow'd in its rage,
As the first-slain slow toppl'd to his fall.
" O King of Desolation, art thou dead ?"
Thought Max, and laughing, heart and lips, leap'd on
The vast, prone trunk. " And have I slain a King ?
" Above his ashes will I build my house—
No slave beneath its pillars, but—a King !"
Max wrought alone, but for a half-breed lad,
With tough, lithe sinews and deep Indian eyes,
Lit with a Gallic sparkle. Max, the lover, found
The labourer's arms grow mightier day by day—
More iron-welded as he slew the trees ;
And with the constant yearning of his heart
Towards little Kate, part of a world away,

His young soul grew and shew'd a virile front,
Full-muscl'd and large statur'd, like his flesh.
Soon the great heaps of brush were builded high,
And like a victor, Max made pause to clear
His battle-field, high strewn with tangl'd dead.
Then roar'd the crackling mountains, and their fires
Met in high heaven, clasping flame with flame.
The thin winds swept a cosmos of red sparks
Across the bleak, midnight sky; and the sun
Walk'd pale behind the resinous, black smoke.
And Max car'd little for the blotted sun,
And nothing for the startl'd, outshone stars;
For Love, once set within a lover's breast,
Has its own Sun—its own peculiar sky,
All one great daffodil—on which do lie
The sun, the moon, the stars—all seen at once,
And never setting; but all shining straight
Into the faces of the trinity,—
The one belov'd, the lover, and sweet Love!
It was not all his own, the axe-stirr'd waste.
In these new days men spread about the earth,
With wings at heel—and now the settler hears,
While yet his axe rings on the primal woods,
The shrieks of engines rushing o'er the wastes;
Nor parts his kind to hew his fortunes out.
And as one drop glides down the unknown rock
And the bright-threaded stream leaps after it,
With welded billions, so the settler finds
His solitary footsteps beaten out,
With the quick rush of panting, human waves
Upheav'd by throbs of angry poverty,

And driven by keen blasts of hunger, from
Their native strands—so stern, so dark, so dear !
O, then, to see the troubl'd, groaning waves,
Throb down to peace in kindly, valley beds ;
Their turbid bosoms clearing in the calm
Of sun-ey'd Plenty—till the stars and moon,
The blessed sun himself, has leave to shine
And laugh in their dark hearts ! So shanties grew
Other than his amid the blacken'd stumps ;
And children ran with little twigs and leaves
And flung them, shouting, on the forest pyres,
Where burn'd the forest kings—and in the glow
Paus'd men and women when the day was done.
There the lean weaver ground anew his axe,
Nor backward look'd upon the vanish'd loom,
But forward to the ploughing of his fields ;
And to the rose of Plenty in the cheeks
Of wife and children—nor heeded much the pangs
Of the rous'd muscles tuning to new work.
The pallid clerk look'd on his blister'd palms
And sigh'd and smil'd, but girded up his loins
And found new vigour as he felt new hope.
The lab'rer with train'd muscles, grim and grave,
Look'd at the ground and wonder'd in his soul,
What joyous anguish stirr'd his darken'd heart,
At the mere look of the familiar soil,
And found his answer in the words—" *Mine own !*"
Then came smooth-coated men, with eager eyes,
And talk'd of steamers on the cliff-bound lakes ;
And iron tracks across the prairie lands ;
And mills to crush the quartz of wealthy hills ;

A LOVE STORY.

And mills to saw the great, wide-arm'd trees;
And mills to grind the singing stream of grain;
And with such busy clamour mingled still
The throbbing music of the bold, bright Axe—
The steel tongue of the Present, and the wail
Of falling forests—voices of the Past.
Max, social-soul'd, and with his practised thews,
Was happy, boy-like, thinking much of Kate,
And speaking of her to the women-folk;
Who, mostly, happy in new honeymoons
Of hope themselves, were ready still to hear
The thrice told tale of Katie's sunny eyes
And Katie's yellow hair, and household ways:
And heard so often, " There shall stand our home—
" On yonder slope, with vines about the door !"
That the good wives were almost made to see
The snowy walls, deep porches, and the gleam
Of Katie's garments flitting through the rooms;
And the black slope all bristling with burn'd stumps
Was known amongst them all as " Max's House."

    O, Love builds on the azure sea,
      And Love builds on the golden sand;
    And Love builds on the rose-wing'd cloud,
      And sometimes Love builds on the land.

    O, if Love build on sparkling sea—
      And if Love build on golden strand—

And if Love build on rosy cloud—
To Love these are the solid land.

O, Love will build his lily walls,
  And Love his pearly roof will rear,—
On cloud or land, or mist or sea—
  Love's solid land is everywhere !

Part III.

The great farm house of Malcolm Graem stood
Square shoulder'd and peak roof'd upon a hill,
With many windows looking everywhere ;
So that no distant meadow might lie hid,
Nor corn-field hide its gold—nor lowing herd
Browse in far pastures, out of Malcolm's ken.
He lov'd to sit, grim, grey, and somewhat stern,
And thro' the smoke-clouds from his short clay pipe
Look out upon his riches ; while his thoughts
Swung back and forth between the bleak, stern past,
And the near future, for his life had come
To that close balance, when, a pendulum,
The memory swings between the " Then" and " Now";
His seldom speech ran thus two diff'rent ways :
" When I was but a laddie, thus I did";

Or, "Katie, in the Fall I'll see to build
"Such fences or such sheds about the place;
"And next year, please the Lord, another barn."
Katie's gay garden foam'd about the walls,
'Leagur'd the prim-cut modern sills, and rush'd
Up the stone walls—and broke on the peak'd roof.
And Katie's lawn was like a Poet's sward,
Velvet and sheer and di'monded with dew;
For such as win their wealth most aptly take
Smooth, urban ways and blend them with their own;
And Katie's dainty raiment was as fine
As the smooth, silken petals of the rose;
And her light feet, her nimble mind and voice,
In city schools had learn'd the city's ways,
And grafts upon the healthy, lovely vine
They shone, eternal blossoms 'mid the fruit.
For Katie had her sceptre in her hand
And wielded it right queenly there and here,
In dairy, store-room, kitchen—ev'ry spot
Where women's ways were needed on the place.
And Malcolm took her through his mighty fields,
And taught her lore about the change of crops;
And how to see a handsome furrow plough'd;
And how to choose the cattle for the mart;
And how to know a fair day's work when done;
And where to plant young orchards; for he said,
"God sent a lassie, but I need a son—
"Bethankit for His mercies all the same."
And Katie, when he said it, thought of Max—
Who had been gone two winters and two springs,
And sigh'd, and thought, "Would he not be your son?"

But all in silence, for she had too much
Of the firm will of Malcolm in her soul
To think of shaking that deep-rooted rock;
But hop'd the crystal current of his love
For his one child, increasing day by day,
Might fret with silver lip, until it wore
Such channels thro' the rock, that some slight stroke
Of circumstance might crumble down the stone.
The wooer, too, had come, Max prophesied;
Reputed wealthy; with the azure eyes
And Saxon-gilded locks—the fair, clear face,
And stalwart form that most women love.
And with the jewels of some virtues set
On his broad brow. With fires within his soul
He had the wizard skill to fetter down
To that mere pink, poetic, nameless glow,
That need not fright a flake of snow away—
But if unloos'd, could melt an adverse rock
Marrow'd with iron, frowning in his way.
And Malcolm balanc'd him by day and night;
And with his grey-ey'd shrewdness partly saw
He was not one for Kate; but let him come,
And in chance moments thought: "Well, let it be—
" They make a bonnie pair—he knows the ways
" Of men and things: can hold the gear I give,
" And, if the lassie wills it, let it be."
And then, upstarting from his midnight sleep,
With hair erect and sweat upon his brow,
Such as no labor e'er had beaded there;
Would cry aloud, wide-staring thro' the dark—
" Nay, nay; she shall not wed him—rest in peace."

Then fully waking, grimly laugh and say :
"Why did I speak and answer when none spake?"
But still lie staring, wakeful, through the shades ;
List'ning to the silence, and beating still
The ball of Alfred's merits to and fro—
Saying, between the silent arguments :
" But would the mother like it, could she know ?
" I would there was a way to ring a lad
" Like silver coin, and so find out the true ;
" But Kate shall say him ' Nay' or say him ' Yea'
" At her own will." And Katie said him " Nay,"
In all the maiden, speechless, gentle ways
A woman has. But Alfred only laugh'd
To his own soul, and said in his wall'd mind :
" O, Kate, were I a lover, I might feel
" Despair flap o'er my hopes with raven wings ;
" Because thy love is giv'n to other love.
" And did I love—unless I gain'd thy love,
" I would disdain the golden hair, sweet lips,
" Air-blown form and true violet eyes ;
" Nor crave the beauteous lamp without the flame ;
" Which in itself would light a charnel house.
" Unlov'd and loving, I would find the cure
" Of Love's despair in nursing Love's disdain—
" Disdain of lesser treasure than the whole.
" One cares not much to place against the wheel
" A diamond lacking flame—nor loves to pluck
" A rose with all its perfume cast abroad
" To the bosom of the gale. Not I, in truth !
" If all man's days are three score years and ten,
" He needs must waste them not, but nimbly seize

" The bright consummate blossom that his will
" Calls for most loudly. Gone, long gone the days
" When Love within my soul for ever stretch'd
" Fierce hands of flame, and here and there I found
" A blossom fitted for him—all up-fill'd
" With love as with clear dew—they had their hour
" And burn'd to ashes with him, as he droop'd
" In his own ruby fires. No Phœnix he,
" To rise again because of Katie's eyes,
" On dewy wings, from ashes such as his !
" But now, another Passion bids me forth,
" To crown him with the fairest I can find,
" And makes me lover—not of Katie's face,
" But of her father's riches ! O, high fool,
" Who feels the faintest pulsing of a wish
" And fails to feed it into lordly life !
" So that, when stumbling back to Mother Earth,
" His freezing lip may curl in cold disdain
" Of those poor, blighted fools who starward stare
" For that fruition, nipp'd and scanted here.
" And, while the clay, o'ermasters all his blood—
" And he can feel the dust knit with his flesh—
" He yet can say to them, ' Be ye content ;
" ' I tasted perfect fruitage thro' my life,
" ' Lighted all lamps of passion, till the oil
" ' Fail'd from their wicks ; and now, O now, I know
" ' There is no Immortality could give
" ' Such boon as this—to simply cease to be !
" ' *There* lies your Heaven, O ye dreaming slaves,
" ' If ye would only live to make it so ;
" ' Nor paint upon the blue skies lying shades

"'Of—*what is not.* Wise, wise and strong the man
"' Who poisons that fond haunter of the mind,
"' Craving for a hereafter with deep draughts
"' Of wild delights—so fiery, fierce, and strong,
"' That when their dregs are deeply, deeply drain'd,
"' What once was blindly crav'd of purblind Chance,
"' Life, life eternal—throbbing thro' all space,
"' Is strongly loath'd—and with his face in dust,
"' Man loves his only Heav'n—six feet of Earth !'
" So, Katie, tho' your blue eyes say me 'Nay,'
" My pangs of love for gold must needs be fed,
" And shall be, Katie, if I know my mind."
Events were winds close nest'ling in the sails
Of Alfred's bark, all blowing him direct
To his wish'd harbour. On a certain day,
All set about with roses and with fire ;
One of three days of heat which frequent slip,
Like triple rubies, in between the sweet,
Mild, emerald days of summer, Katie went,
Drawn by a yearning for the ice-pale blooms,
Natant and shining—firing all the bay
With angel fires built up of snow and gold.
She found the bay close pack'd with groaning logs,
Prison'd between great arms of close hing'd wood.
All cut from Malcolm's forests in the west,
And floated hither to his noisy mills ;
And all stamp'd with the potent "G." and "M.,"
Which much he lov'd to see upon his goods,
The silent courtiers owning him their king.
Out clear beyond the rustling ricebeds sang,
And the cool lilies starr'd the shadow'd wave.

"This is a day for lily-love," said Kate,
While she made bare the lilies of her feet;
And sang a lily-song that Max had made,
That spoke of lilies—always meaning Kate.

"While Lady of the silver'd lakes,
Chaste Goddess of the sweet, still shrines.
   The jocund river fitful makes,
By sudden, deep gloom'd brakes,
Close shelter'd by close weft and woof of vine,
Spilling a shadow gloomy-rich as wine,
Into the silver throne where thou dost sit,
Thy silken leaves all dusky round thee knit!

"Mild soul of the unsalted wave!
   White bosom holding golden fire!
Deep as some ocean-hidden cave
   Are fix'd the roots of thy desire,
Thro' limpid currents stealing up,
And rounding to the pearly cup
   Thou dost desire,
With all thy trembling heart of sinless fire,
   But to be fill'd
   With dew distill'd
From clear, fond skies, that in their gloom
Hold, floating high, thy sister moon,

Pale chalice of a sweet perfume,
Whiter-breasted than a dove—
To thee the dew is—love!"

Kate bared her little feet, and pois'd herself
On the first log close grating on the shore ;
And with bright eyes of laughter, and wild hair—
A flying wind of gold—from log to log
Sped, laughing as they wallow'd in her track,
Like brown-scal'd monsters rolling, as her foot
Spurn'd each in turn with its rose-white sole.
A little island, out in middlewave,
With its green shoulder held the great drive brac'd
Between it and the mainland ; here it was
The silver lilies drew her with white smiles ;
And as she touch'd the last great log of all,
It reel'd, upstarting, like a column brac'd,
A second on the wave—and when it plung'd
Rolling upon the froth and sudden foam,
Katie had vanish'd, and with angry grind
The vast logs roll'd together,—nor a lock
Of drifting, yellow hair—an upflung hand,
Told where the rich man's chiefest treasure sank
Under his wooden wealth. But Alfred, laid
With pipe and book upon the shady marge
Of the cool isle, saw all, and seeing hurl'd
Himself, and hardly knew it, on the logs ;
By happy chance a shallow lapp'd the isle
On this green bank ; and when his iron arms
Dash'd the bark'd monsters, as frail stems of rice,

A little space apart, the soft, slow tide
But reach'd his chest, and in a flash he saw
Kate's yellow hair, and by it drew her up,
And lifting her aloft, cried out, " O, Kate !"
And once again said, " Katie ! is she dead ?"
For like the lilies broken by the rough
And sudden riot of the armor'd logs,
Kate lay upon his hands ; and now the logs
Clos'd in upon him, nipping his great chest,
Nor could he move to push them off again
For Katie in his arms. "And now," he said,
" If none should come, and any wind arise
" To weld these woody monsters 'gainst the isle,
" I shall be crack'd like any broken twig ;
" And as it is, I know not if I die,
" For I am hurt—aye, sorely, sorely hurt !"
Then look'd on Katie's lily face, and said,
" Dead, dead or living ? Why, an even chance.
" O lovely bubble on a troubl'd sea,
" I would not thou shoulds't lose thyself again
" In the black ocean whence thy life emerg'd,
" But skyward steal on gales as soft as love,
" And hang in some bright rainbow overhead,
" If only such bright rainbow spann'd the earth."
Then shouted loudly, till the silent air
Rous'd like a frighten'd bird, and on its wings
Caught up his cry and bore it to the farm.
There Malcolm, leaping from his noontide sleep,
Upstarted as at midnight, crying out,
"She shall not wed him—rest you, wife, in peace !"
They found him, Alfred, haggard-ey'd and faint,

But holding Katie ever towards the sun,
Unhurt, and waking in the fervent heat.
And now it came that Alfred being sick
Of his sharp hurts and tended by them both,
With what was like to love, being born of thanks,
Had choice of hours most politic to woo,
And used his deed as one might use the sun,
To ripen unmellow'd fruit; and from the core
Of Katie's gratitude hop'd yet to nurse
A flow'r all to his liking—Katie's love.
But Katie's mind was like the plain, broad shield
Of a table di'mond, nor had a score of sides;
And in its shield, so precious and so plain,
Was cut, thro' all its clear depths—Max's name.
And so she said him "Nay" at last, in words
Of such true sounding silver, that he knew
He might not win her at the present hour,
But smil'd and thought—" I go, and come again !
" Then shall we see. Our three-score years and ten
" Are mines of treasure, if we hew them deep,
" Nor stop too long in choosing out our tools !"

Part IV.

From his far wigwam sprang the strong North Wind
And rush'd with war-cry down the steep ravines,
And wrestl'd with the giants of the woods;
And with his ice-club beat the swelling crests
Of the deep watercourses into death,
And with his chill foot froze the whirling leaves

Of dun and gold and fire in icy banks ;
And smote the tall reeds to the harden'd earth ;
And sent his whistling arrows o'er the plains,
Scatt'ring the ling'ring herds—and sudden paus'd
When he had frozen all the running streams,
And hunted with his war-cry all the things
That breath'd about the woods, or roam'd the bleak
Bare prairies swelling to the mournful sky.
" White squaw," he shouted, troubl'd in his soul,
" I slew the dead, wrestl'd with naked chiefs
" Unplum'd before, scalped of their leafy plumes ;
" I bound sick rivers in cold thongs of death,
" And shot my arrows over swooning plains,
" Bright with the Paint of death—and lean and bare.
" And all the braves of my loud tribe will mock
" And point at me—when our great chief, the Sun,
" Relights his Council fire in the moon
" Of Budding Leaves." " Ugh, ugh ! he is a brave !
" He fights with squaws and takes the scalps of babes !
" And the least wind will blow his calumet—
" Fill'd with the breath of smallest flow'rs—across
" The war-paint on my face, and pointing with
" His small, bright pipe, that never moved a spear
" Of bearded rice, cry, ' Ugh ! he slays the dead !'
" O, my white squaw, come from thy wigwam grey,
" Spread thy white blanket on the twice-slain dead ;
" And hide them, ere the waking of the Sun !"

High grew the snow beneath the low-hung sky,
And all was silent in the Wilderness ;

In trance of stillness Nature heard her God
Rebuilding her spent fires, and veil'd her face
While the Great Worker brooded o'er His work.

" Bite deep and wide, O Axe, the tree,
What doth thy bold voice promise me?"

" I promise thee all joyous things,
That furnish forth the lives of kings!

" For ev'ry silver ringing blow,
Cities and palaces shall grow!"

" Bite deep and wide, O Axe, the tree,
Tell wider prophecies to me."

" When rust hath gnaw'd me deep and red,
A nation strong shall lift his head!

" His crown the very Heav'ns shall smite,
Æons shall build him in his might!"

"Bite deep and wide, O Axe, the tree;
Bright Seer, help on thy prophecy!"

Max smote the snow-weigh'd tree and lightly laugh'd.
"See, friend," he cried to one that look'd and smil'd,
"My axe and I—we do immortal tasks—
We build up nations—this my axe and I!"
"O," said the other with a cold, short smile,
"Nations are not immortal! is there now
"One nation thron'd upon the sphere of earth,
"That walk'd with the first Gods, and saw
"The budding world unfold its slow-leav'd flow'r?
"Nay; it is hardly theirs to leave behind
"Ruins so eloquent, that the hoary sage
"Can lay his hand upon their stones, and say:
"'These once were thrones!' The lean, lank lion peals
"His midnight thunders over lone, red plains,
"Long-ridg'd and crested on their dusty waves,
"With fires from moons red-hearted as the sun;
"And deep re-thunders all the earth to him.
"For, far beneath the flame-fleck'd, shifting sands,
"Below the roots of palms, and under stones
"Of younger ruins, thrones, tow'rs and cities
"Honeycomb the earth. The high, solemn walls
"Of hoary ruins—their foundings all unknown
"(But to the round-ey'd worlds that walk
"In the blank paths of Space and blanker Chance).
"At whose stones young mountains wonder, and the seas'
"New-silv'ring, deep-set valleys pause and gaze;

" Are rear'd upon old shrines, whose very Gods
" Were dreams to the shrine-builders, of a time
" They caught in far-off flashes—as the child
" Half thinks he can remember how one came
" And took him in her hand and shew'd him that
" He thinks, she call'd the sun. Proud ships rear high
" On ancient billows that have torn the roots
" Of cliffs, and bitten at the golden lips
" Of firm, sleek beaches, till they conquer'd all,
" And sow'd the reeling earth with salted waves.
" Wrecks plunge, prow foremost, down still, solemn slopes,
" And bring their dead crews to as dead a quay ;
" Some city built before that ocean grew,
" By silver drops from many a floating cloud,
" By icebergs bellowing in their throes of death,
" By lesser seas toss'd from their rocking cups,
" And leaping each to each ; by dew-drops flung
" From painted sprays, whose weird leaves and flow'rs
" Are moulded for new dwellers on the earth,
" Printed in hearts of mountains and of mines.
" Nations immortal ? where the well-trimm'd lamps
" Of long-past ages, when Time seem'd to pause
" On smooth, dust-blotted graves that, like the tombs
" Of monarchs, held dead bones and sparkling gems ?
" She saw no glimmer on the hideous ring
" Of the black clouds ; no stream of sharp, clear light
" From those great torches, pass'd into the black
" Of deep oblivion. She seem'd to watch, but she
" Forgot her long-dead nations. When she stirr'd
" Her vast limbs in the dawn that forc'd its fire
" Up the black East, and saw the imperious red

" Burst over virgin dews and budding flow'rs,
" She still forgot her molder'd thrones and kings,
" Her sages and their torches, and their Gods,
" And said, ' This is my birth—my primal day !'
" She dream'd new Gods, and rear'd them other shrines,
" Planted young nations, smote a feeble flame
" From sunless flint, re-lit the torch of mind ;
" Again she hung her cities on the hills,
" Built her rich towers, crown'd her kings again,
" And with the sunlight on her awful wings
" Swept round the flow'ry cestus of the earth,
" And said, ' I build for Immortality !'
" Her vast hand rear'd her tow'rs, her shrines, her thrones;
" The ceaseless sweep of her tremendous wings
" Still beat them down and swept their dust abroad ;
" Her iron finger wrote on mountain sides
" Her deeds and prowess—and her own soft plume
" Wore down the hills ! Again drew darkly on
" A night of deep forgetfulness ; once more
" Time seem'd to pause upon forgotten graves—
" Once more a young dawn stole into her eyes—
" Again her broad wings stirr'd, and fresh clear airs,
" Blew the great clouds apart ;—again Time said,
" ' This is my birth—my deeds and handiwork
" ' Shall be immortal.' Thus and so dream on
" Fool'd nations, and thus dream their dullard sons.
" Naught is immortal save immortal—Death !"
Max paus'd and smil'd : " O, preach such gospel, friend,
" To all but lovers who most truly love ;
" For *them*, their gold-wrought scripture glibly reads,
" All else is mortal but immortal—Love !"

A LOVE STORY.

"Fools! fools!" his friend said, "most immortal fools!—
"But pardon, pardon, for, perchance, you love?"
"Yes," said Max, proudly smiling, "thus do I
"Possess the world and feel eternity!"
Dark laughter blacken'd in the other's eyes:
"Eternity! why, did such Iris arch
"Ent'ring our worm-bored planet, never liv'd
"One woman true enough such tryst to keep!"
"I'd swear by Kate," said Max; "and then, I had
"A mother, and my father swore by her."
"By Kate? Ah, that were lusty oath, indeed!
"Some other man will look into her eyes,
"And swear me roundly, 'By true Catherine!'
"And Troilus swore by Cressèd—so they say."
"You never knew my Kate," said Max, and pois'd
His axe again on high, "But let it pass—
"You are too subtle for me; argument
"Have I none to oppose yours with—but this,
"Get you a Kate, and let her sunny eyes
"Dispel the doubting darkness in your soul."
"And have not I a Kate? pause, friend, and see.
"She gave me this faint shadow of herself
"The day I slipp'd the watch-star of our loves—
"A ring—upon her hand—she loves me, too;
"Yet tho' her eyes be suns, no Gods are they
"To give me worlds, or make me feel a tide
"Of strong Eternity set towards my soul;
"And tho' she loves me, yet am I content
"To know she loves me by the hour—the year—
"Perchance the second—as all women love."
The bright axe falter'd in the air, and ripp'd

Down the rough bark, and bit the drifted snow,
For Max's arm fell, wither'd in its strength,
'Long by his side. " Your Kate," he said ; " your Kate!"
" Yes, mine, while holds her mind that way, my Kate ;
" I sav'd her life, and had her love for thanks ;
" Her father is Malcolm Graem—Max, my friend,
" You pale ! what sickness seizes on your soul ?
Max laugh'd, and swung his bright axe high again :
" Stand back a pace—a too far reaching blow
" Might level your false head with yon prone trunk—
" Stand back and listen while I say, " You lie !
" That is my Katie's face upon your breast,
" But 'tis my Katie's love lives in my breast—
" Stand back, I say ! my axe is heavy, and
" Might chance to cleave a liar's brittle skull.
" Your Kate ! your Kate ! your Kate !—hark, how the
" Mock at your lie with all their woody tongues. [woods,
" O, silence, ye false echoes ! not his Kate
" But mine—I'm certain I will have your life !"
All the blue heav'n was dead in Max's eyes ;
Doubt-wounded lay Kate's image in his heart,
And could not rise to pluck the sharp spear out.
" Well, strike, mad fool," said Alfred, somewhat pale ;
" I have no weapon but these naked hands."
" Aye, but," said Max, " you smote my naked heart !
" O shall I slay him ?—Satan, answer me—
" I cannot call on God for answer here.
" O Kate—!"
A voice from God came thro' the silent woods
And answer'd him—for suddenly a wind
Caught the great tree-tops, coned with high-pil'd snow,

And smote them to and fro, while all the air
Was sudden fill'd with busy drifts, and high
White pillars whirl'd amid the naked trunks,
And harsh, loud groans, and smiting, sapless boughs
Made hellish clamour in the quiet place.
With a shrill shriek of tearing fibres, rock'd
The half-hewn tree above his fated head ;
And, tott'ring, asked the sudden blast, "Which way ?"
And, answ'ring its windy arms, crash'd and broke
Thro' other lacing boughs, with one loud roar
Of woody thunder ; all its pointed boughs
Pierc'd the deep snow—its round and mighty corpse,
Bark-flay'd and shudd'ring, quiver'd into death.
And Max—as some frail, wither'd reed, the sharp
And piercing branches caught at him,
As hands in a death-throe, and beat him to the earth—
And the dead tree upon its slayer lay.
"Yet hear we much of Gods ;—if such there be,
"They play at games of chance with thunderbolts,"
Said Alfred, "else on me this doom had come.
"This seals my faith in deep and dark unfaith !
"Now Katie, are you mine, for Max is dead—
"Or will be soon, imprison'd by those boughs,
"Wounded and torn, sooth'd by the deadly palms
"Of the white, trait'rous frost ; and buried then
"Under the snows that fill those vast, grey clouds,
"Low-sweeping on the fretted forest roof.
"And Katie shall believe you false—not dead ;
"False, false !—And I ? O, she shall find me true—
"True as a fabl'd devil to the soul
"He longs for with the heat of all hell's fires.

"These myths serve well for simile, I see.
" And yet—Down, Pity ! knock not at my breast,
" Nor grope about for that dull stone my heart ;
" I'll stone thee with it, Pity ! Get thee hence,
" Pity, I'll strangle thee with naked hands ;
" For thou dost bear upon thy downy breast
" Remorse, shap'd like a serpent, and her fangs
" Might dart at me and pierce my marrow thro'.
" Hence, beggar, hence—and keep with fools, I say !
" He bleeds and groans ! Well, Max, thy God or mine
" Blind Chance, here play'd the butcher—'twas not I.
" Down, hands ! ye shall not lift his fall'n head ;
" What cords tug at ye ? What ? Ye'd pluck him up
" And staunch his wounds ? There rises in my breast
" A strange, strong giant, throwing wide his arms
" And bursting all the granite of my heart !
" How like to quiv'ring flesh a stone may feel !
" Why, it has pangs ! I'll none of them. I know
" Life is too short for anguish and for hearts—
" So I wrestle with thee, giant ! and my will
" Turns the thumb, and thou shalt take the knife.
" Well done ! I'll turn thee on the arena dust,
" And look on thee—What ? thou wert Pity's self,
" Stol'n in my breast ; and I have slaughter'd thee—
" But hist—where hast thou hidden thy fell snake,
" Fire-fang'd Remorse ? Not in my breast, I know,
" For all again is chill and empty there,
" And hard and cold—the granite knitted up.
" So lie there, Max—poor fond and simple Max,
" 'Tis well thou diest ; earth's children should not call
" Such as thee father—let them ever be

" Father'd by rogues and villians, fit to cope
" With the foul dragon Chance, and the black knaves
" Who swarm'd in loathsome masses in the dust.
" True Max, lie there, and slumber into death."

Part V.

Said the high hill, in the morning : " Look on me—
" Behold, sweet earth, sweet sister sky, behold
" The red flames on my peaks, and how my pines
" Are cressets of pure gold ; my quarried scars
" Of black crevase and shadow-fill'd canon,
" Are trac'd in silver mist. How on my breast
" Hang the soft purple fringes of the night ;
" Close to my shoulder droops the weary moon,
" Dove-pale, into the crimson surf the sun
" Drives up before his prow ; and blackly stands
" On my slim, loftiest peak, an eagle, with
" His angry eyes set sunward, while his cry
" Falls fiercely back from all my ruddy heights ;
" And his bald eaglets, in their bare, broad nest,
" Shrill pipe their angry echoes : " ' Sun, arise,
" ' And show me that pale dove, beside her nest,
" ' Which I shall strike with piercing beak and tear
" ' With iron talons for my hungry young.' "
And that mild dove, secure for yet a space,
Half waken'd, turns her ring'd and glossy neck
To watch dawn's ruby pulsing on her breast,
And see the first bright golden motes slip down

The gnarl'd trunks about her leaf-deep nest,
Nor sees nor fears the eagle on the peak.

"Aye, lassie, sing—I'll smoke my pipe the while,
"And let it be a simple, bonnie song,
"Such as an old, plain man can gather in
"His dulling ear, and feel it slipping thro'
"The cold, dark, stony places of his heart."
"Yes, sing, sweet Kate," said Alfred in her ear;
"I often heard you singing in my dreams
"When I was far away the winter past."
So Katie on the moonlit window lean'd,
And in the airy silver of her voice
Sang of the tender, blue "Forget-me-not."

> Could every blossom find a voice,
>   And sing a strain to me;
> I know where I would place my choice,
>   Which my delight should be.
> I would not choose the lily tall,
>   The rose from musky grot;
> But I would still my minstrel call
>   The blue "Forget-me-not!"
>
> And I on mossy bank would lie
>   Of brooklet, ripp'ling clear;
> And she of the sweet azure eye,
>   Close at my list'ning ear,
> Should sing into my soul a strain
>   Might never be forgot—
> So rich with joy, so rich with pain
>   The blue "Forget-me-not!"

Ah, ev'ry blossom hath a tale
 With silent grace to tell,
From rose that reddens to the gale
 To modest heather bell;
But O, the flow'r in ev'ry heart
 That finds a sacred spot
To bloom, with azure leaves apart,
 Is the "Forget-me-not!"

Love plucks it from the mosses green
 When parting hours are nigh,
And places it loves palms between,
 With many an ardent sigh;
And bluely up from grassy graves
 In some lov'd churchyard spot,
It glances tenderly and waves,
 The dear "Forget-me-not!"

And with the faint last cadence, stole a glance
At Malcolm's soften'd face—a bird-soft touch
Let flutter on the rugged silver snarls
Of his thick locks, and laid her tender lips
A second on the iron of his hand.
"And did you ever meet," he sudden ask'd
Of Alfred, sitting pallid in the shade,
"Out by yon unco place, a lad,—a lad
"Nam'd Maxwell Gordon; tall, and straight, and strong;
"About my size, I take it, when a lad?"
And Katie at the sound of Max's name,
First spoken for such space by Malcolm's lips,
Trembl'd and started, and let down her brow,
Hiding its sudden rose on Malcolm's arm.

"Max Gordon? Yes. Was he a friend of yours?"
"No friend of mine, but of the lassie's here—
"How comes he on? I wager he's a drone,
"And never will put honey in the hive."
"No drone." said Alfred, laughing; "when I left
"He and his axe were quarr'ling with the woods
"And making forests reel—love steels a lover's arm"
O, blush that stole from Katie's swelling heart,
And with its hot rose brought the happy dew
Into her hidden eyes. "Aye, aye! is that the way?"
Said Malcolm, smiling. "Who may be his love?"
"In that he is a somewhat simple soul,
"Why, I suppose he loves—" he paused, and Kate
Look'd up with two "forget-me-nots" for eyes,
With eager jewels in their centres set
Of happy, happy tears, and Alfred's heart
Became a closer marble than before.
"—Why I suppose he loves—his lawful wife."
"His wife! his wife!" said Malcolm, in a maze,
And laid his heavy hand on Katie's head;
"Did you two play me false, my little lass?
"Speak and I'll pardon! Katie, lassie, what?"
"He has a wife," said Alfred, "lithe and bronz'd,
"An Indian woman, comelier than her kind;
"And on her knee a child with yellow locks,
"And lake-like eyes of mystic Indian brown.
"And so you knew him? He is doing well."
"False, false!" said Katie, lifting up her head.
"O, you know not the Max my father means!"
"He came from yonder farm-house on the slope."
"Some other Max—we speak not of the same."

" He has a red mark on his temple set."
" It matters not—'tis not the Max we know."
" He wears a turquoise ring slung round his neck."
" And many wear them—they are common stones."
" His mother's ring—her name was Helen Wynde."
" And there be many Helens who have sons."
" O Katie, credit me—it is the man."
" O not the man! Why, you have never told
" Us of the true soul that the true Max has;
" The Max we know has such a soul, I know."
" How know you that," my foolish little lass?
Said Malcolm, a storm of anger bound
Within his heart, like Samson with green withs—
" Belike it is the false young cur we know!"
" No, no," said Katie, simply, and low-voic'd;
" If he were traitor I must needs be false,
" For long ago love melted our two hearts,
" And time has moulded those two hearts in one,
" And he is true since I am faithful still."
She rose and parted, trembling as she went,
Feeling the following steel of Alfred's eyes,
And with the icy hand of scorn'd mistrust
Searching about the pulses of her heart—
Feeling for Max's image in her breast.
" To-night she conquers Doubt; to-morrow's noon
" His following soldiers sap the golden wall,
" And I shall enter and possess the fort,"
Said Alfred, in his mind. " O Katie, child,
" Wilt thou be Nemesis, with yellow hair,
" To rend my breast? for I do feel a pulse
" Stir when I look into thy pure-barb'd eyes—

"O, am I breeding that false thing, a heart?
"Making my breast all tender for the fangs
"Of sharp Remorse to plunge their hot fire in.
"I am a certain dullard! Let me feel
"But one faint goad, fine as a needle's point,
"And it shall be the spur in my soul's side
"To urge the madd'ning thing across the jags
"And cliffs of life, into the soft embrace
"Of that cold mistress, who is constant too,
"And never flings her lovers from her arms—
"Not Death, for she is still a fruitful wife,
"Her spouse the Dead, and their cold marriage yields
"A million children, born of mould'ring flesh—
"So Death and Flesh live on—immortal they!
"I mean the blank-ey'd queen whose wassail bowl
"Is brimm'd from Lethe, and whose porch is red
"With poppies, as it waits the panting soul—
"She, she alone is great! No scepter'd slave
"Bowing to blind creative giants, she;
"No forces seize her in their strong, mad hands,
"Nor say, "'Do this—be that!'" Were there a God,
"His only mocker, she, great Nothingness!
"And to her, close of kin, yet lover too,
"Flies this large nothing that we call the soul."

"Doth true Love lonely grow?
     Ah, no! ah, no!
Ah, were it only so—
That it alone might show

Its ruddy rose upon its sapful tree,
  Then, then in dewy morn,
  Joy might his brow adorn
With Love's young rose as fair and glad as he."

But with Love's rose doth blow
      Ah, woe ! ah, woe !
Truth with its leaves of snow,
And Pain and Pity grow
 With Love's sweet roses on its sapful tree !
  Love's rose buds not alone,
  But still, but still doth own
A thousand blossoms cypress-hued to see !

Part VI.

" Who curseth Sorrow knows her not at all.
Dark matrix she, from which the human soul
Has its last birth ; whence, with its misty thews,
Close-knitted in her blackness, issues out ;
Strong for immortal toil up such great heights,
As crown o'er crown rise through Eternity,
Without the loud, deep clamour of her wail,
The iron of her hands, the biting brine
Of her black tears ; the Soul but lightly built
Of indeterminate spirit, like a mist
Would lapse to Chaos in soft, gilded dreams,
As mists fade in the gazing of the sun.

Sorrow, dark mother of the soul, arise !
Be crown'd with spheres where thy bless'd children dwell,
Who, but for thee, were not. No lesser seat
Be thine, thou Helper of the Universe,
Than planet on planet pil'd !—thou instrument,
Close-clasp'd within the great Creative Hand !"

———

The Land had put his ruddy gauntlet on,
Of Harvest gold, to dash in Famine's face.
And like a vintage wain, deep dy'd with juice,
The great moon falter'd up the ripe, blue sky,
Drawn by silver stars—like oxen white
And horn'd with rays of light—Down the rich land
Malcolm's small valleys, fill'd with grain, lip-high,
Lay round a lonely hill that fac'd the moon,
And caught the wine-kiss of its ruddy light.
A cusp'd, dark wood caught in its black embrace
The valleys and the hill, and from its wilds,
Spic'd with dark cedars, cried the Whip-poor-will.
A crane, belated, sail'd across the moon ;
On the bright, small, close link'd lakes green islets lay,
Dusk knots of tangl'd vines, or maple boughs,
Or tuft'd cedars, boss'd upon the waves.
The gay, enamell'd children of the swamp
Roll'd a low bass to treble, tinkling notes
Of little streamlets leaping from the woods.
Close to old Malcolm's mills, two wooden jaws
Bit up the water on a sloping floor ;
And here, in season, rush'd the great logs down,

A LOVE STORY.

To seek the river winding on its way.
In a green sheen, smooth as a Naiad's locks,
The water roll'd between the shudd'ring jaws—
Then on the river level roar'd and reel'd—
In ivory-arm'd conflict with itself.
"Look down," said Alfred, "Katie, look and see
"How that but pictures my mad heart to you.
"It tears itself in fighting that mad love
"You swear is hopeless—hopeless—is it so?"
"Ah, yes!" said Katie, "ask me not again."
"But Katie, Max is false; no word has come,
"Nor any sign from him for many months,
"And—he is happy with his Indian wife."
She lifted eyes fair as the fresh grey dawn
With all its dews and promises of sun.
"O, Alfred!—saver of my little life—
"Look in my eyes and read them honestly."
He laugh'd till all the isles and forests laugh'd.
"O simple child! what may the forest flames
"See in the woodland ponds but their own fires?
"And have you, Katie, neither fears nor doubts?'
She, with the flow'r soft pinkness of her palm
Cover'd her sudden tears, then quickly said:
"Fears—never doubts, for true love never doubts."
Then Alfred paus'd a space, as one who holds
A white doe by the throat and searches for
The blade to slay her. "This your answer still—
"You doubt not—doubt not this far love of yours,
"Tho' sworn a false young recreant, Kate, by me?"
"He is as true as I am," Katie said;
"And did I seek for stronger simile,

" I could not find such in the universe !"
" And were he dead ? what, Katie, were he dead—
" A handful of brown dust, a flame blown out—
" What then would love be strongly true to—Naught ?"
" Still true to love my love would be," she said,
And faintly smiling, pointed to the stars.
" O fool !" said Alfred, stirr'd—as craters rock
To their own throes—and over his pale lips
Roll'd flaming stone, his molten heart. " Then, fool—
" Be true to what thou wilt—for he is dead.
" And there have grown this gilded summer past
" Grasses and buds from his unburied flesh.
" I saw him dead. I heard his last, loud cry :
" ' O Kate !' ring thro' the woods ; in truth I did."
She half-raised up a piteous, pleading hand,
Then fell along the mosses at his feet.
" Now will I show I love you, Kate," he said,
" And give you gift of love ; you shall not wake
" To feel the arrow, feather-deep, within
" Your constant heart. For me, I never meant
" To crawl an hour beyond what time I felt
" The strange, fang'd monster that they call Remorse
" Fold round my waken'd heart. The hour has come ;
" And as Love grew, the welded folds of steel
" Slipp'd round in horrid zones. In Love's flaming eyes
" Stared its fell eyeballs, and with Hydra head
" It sank hot fangs in breast, and brow and thigh.
" Come, Kate ! O Anguish is a simple knave
" Whom hucksters could outwit with small trade lies,
" When thus so easily his smarting thralls,
" May flee his knout ! Come, come, my little Kate ;

" The black porch with its fringe of poppies waits—
" A propylaeum hospitably wide.
" No lictors with their fasces at its jaws,
" Its floor as kindly to my fire-vein'd feet
" As to thy silver, lilied, sinless ones.
" O you shall slumber soundly, tho' the white,
" Wild waters pluck the crocus of your hair ;
" And scaly spies stare with round, lightless eyes
" At your small face laid on my stony breast.
" Come, Kate ! I must not have you wake, dear heart,
" To hear you cry, perchance, on your dead Max."
He turn'd her still face close upon his breast,
And with his lips upon her soft, ring'd hair,
Leap'd from the bank, low shelving o'er the knot
Of frantic waters at the long slide's foot.
And as the sever'd waters crash'd and smote
Together once again,—within the wave-
Stunn'd chamber of his ear there peal'd a cry :
" O Kate ! stay, madman ; traitor, stay ! O Kate !"

Max, gaunt as prairie wolves in famine time,
With long drawn sickness, reel'd upon the bank—
Katie, new-rescu'd, waking in his arms.
On the white riot of the waters gleam'd,
The face of Alfred, calm, with close-seal'd eyes,
And blood red on his temple where it smote
The mossy timbers of the groaning slide.
" O God !" said Max, as Katie's opening eyes
Looked up to his, slow budding to a smile

Of wonder and of bliss, " My Kate, my Kate !"
She saw within his eyes a larger soul
Than that light spirit that before she knew,
And read the meaning of his glance and words.
" Do as you will, my Max. I would not keep
" You back with one light-falling finger-tip !"
And cast herself from his large arms upon
The mosses at his feet, and hid her face
That she might not behold what he would do ;
Or lest the terror in her shining eyes
Might bind him to her, and prevent his soul
Work out its greatness ; and her long, wet hair
Drew, mass'd, about her ears, to shut the sound
Of the vex'd waters from her anguish'd brain.
Max look'd upon her, turning as he look'd.
A moment came a voice in Katie's soul :
" Arise, be not dismay'd, arise and look ;
" If he should perish, 'twill be as a God,
" For he would die to save his enemy."
But answer'd her torn heart : " I cannot look—
" I cannot look and see him sob and die
" In those pale, angry arms. O, let me rest
" Blind, blind and deaf until the swift pac'd end.
" My Max ! O God—was that his Katie's name ?"
Like a pale dove, hawk-hunted, Katie ran,
Her fear's beak in her shoulder ; and below,
Where the coil'd waters straighten'd to a stream,
Found Max all bruis'd and bleeding on the bank,
But smiling with man's triumph in his eyes,
When he has on fierce Danger's lion neck
Plac'd his right hand and pluck'd the prey away.

And at his feet lay Alfred, still and white,
A willow's shadow tremb'ling on his face.
" There lies the false, fair devil, O my Kate,
" Who would have parted us, but could not, Kate !"
" But could not, Max," said Katie. " Is he dead ?"
But, swift perusing Max's strange, dear face,
Close clasp'd against his breast—forgot him straight
And ev'ry other evil thing upon
The broad green earth.

Part VII.

Again rang out the music of the axe,
And on the slope, as in his happy dreams,
The home of Max with wealth of drooping vines
On the rude walls, and in the trellis'd porch
Sat Katie, smiling o'er the rich, fresh fields ;
And by her side sat Malcolm, hale and strong ;
Upon his knee a little, smiling child,
Nam'd—Alfred, as the seal of pardon set
Upon the heart of one who sinn'd and woke
To sorrow for his sins—and whom they lov'd
With gracious joyousness—nor kept the dusk
Of his past deeds between their hearts and his.
Malcolm had follow'd with his flocks and herds
When Max and Katie, hand in hand, went out
From his old home ; and now, with slow, grave smile,
He said to Max, who twisted Katie's hair
About his naked arm, bare from his toil :

" It minds me of old times. this house of yours ;
" It stirs my heart to hearken to the axe,
" And hear the windy crash of falling trees ;
" Aye, these fresh forests make an old man young."
" Oh, yes !" said Max, with laughter in his eyes ;
" And I do truly think that Eden bloom'd
" Deep in the heart of tall, green maple groves,
" With sudden scents of pine from mountain sides
" And prairies with their breasts against the skies.
" And Eve was only little Katie's height."
" Hoot, lad ! you speak as ev'ry Adam speaks
" About his bonnie Eve ; but what says Kate ?"
" O Adam had not Max's soul," she said ;
" And these wild woods and plains are fairer far
" Than Eden's self. O bounteous mothers they !
" Beck'ning pale starvelings with their fresh, green hands,
" And with their ashes mellowing the earth,
" That she may yield her increase willingly.
" I would not change these wild and rocking woods,
" Dotted by little homes of unbirk'd trees,
" Where dwell the fleers from the waves of want,—
" For the smooth sward of selfish Eden bowers,
" Nor—Max for Adam, if I knew my mind !"

OLD SPENSE.

You've seen his place, I reckon, friend?
  'Twas rather kind ov tryin',
The way he made the dollars fly,
  Such gimcrack things a-buyin'—
    He spent a big share ov a fortin'
    On pesky things that went a snortin'

And hollerin' over all the fields,
  And ploughin' ev'ry furrow;
We sort ov felt discouraged, for
  Spense wusn't one to borrow;
    An' wus—the old chap wouldn't lend
    A cent's wuth to his dearest friend!

Good land! the neighbours seed to wunst
  Them snortin', screamin' notions
Wus jest enough tew drown the yearth
  In wrath, like roarin' oceans,
    "An' guess'd the Lord would give old Spense
    Blue fits for fightin' Pruvidence!"

Spense wus thet harden'd; when the yearth
  Wus like a bak'd pertater;
Instead ov prayin' hard fur rain,

He fetched an irrigator.
"The wicked flourish like green bays!"
Sed folks for comfort in them days.

I will allow his place was grand,
　With not a stump upon it,
The loam wus jest as rich an' black
　Es school ma'am's velvet bunnit;
　　But tho' he flourish'd, folks all know'd
　　What spiritooal ear-marks he show'd.

Spense had a notion in his mind,
　Ef some poor human grapples
With pesky worms thet eat his vines,
　An' spile his summer apples,
　　It don't seem enny kind ov sense
　　Tew call that "cheekin' Pruvidence!"

An' ef a chap on Sabbath sees
　A thunder cloud a-strayin'
Above his fresh cut clover an'
　Gets down tew steddy prayin',
　　An' tries tew shew the Lord's mistake,
　　Instead ov tacklin' tew his rake,

He ain't got enny kind ov show
　Tew talk ov chast'ning trials;
When thet thar thunder cloud lets down
　It's sixty billion vials;
　　No! when it looks tew rain on hay,
　　First take yer rake an' then yer pray!

OLD SPENSE.

Old Spense was one ov them thar chaps
  Thet in this life of tussle,
An' rough-an'-tumble, sort ov set
  A mighty store on muscle ;
    B'liev'd in hustlin' in the crop,
    An' prayin' on the last load top !

An' yet he hed his p'ints—his heart
  Wus builded sort ov spacious ;
An' solid—ev'ry beam an' plank,
  An', Stranger, now, veracious.
    A wore-out hoss he never shot,
    But turn'd him in the clover lot !

I've seed up tew the meetin' house,
  The winkin' an' the nudgin',
When preacher sed, " No doubt that Dives
  Been drefful mean an' grudgin' ;
    Tew church work seal'd his awful fate
    Whar thar ain't no foolin' with the gate ;"

I mind the preacher met old Spense,
  Beneath the maples laggin',
The day was hot, an' he'd a pile
  Ov 'cetrees in his waggin' ;
    A sack of flour, a hansum hog,
    Sum butter and his terrier dog.

Preacher, he halted up his hoss,
  Ask'd for Miss Spense an' Deely,
Tew limber up his tongue a mite,

And sez right slick an' mealy :
  "Brother, I really want tew know
  Hev you got religion? Samson, whoa!"

Old Spense, he bit a noble chaw,
  An' sort ov meditated ;
Samson he nibbl'd at the grass,
  An' preacher smil'd and waited ;
    Ye'd see it writ upon his face—
    "I've got Spense in a tightsome place!"

The old man curl'd his whip-lash round
  An alto-vic'd muskitter,
Preacher, sort ov triumphant, strok'd
  His ornary old critter.
    Spense p'ints tew flour, an' hog, an' jar,
    Sez he, "I've got religion thar!

"Them's goin' down tew Spinkses place,
  Whar old man Spinks is stayin' ;
The bank he dealt at bust last month,
  An' folks is mostly sayin' :
    Him bein' ag'd, an' poor, an' sick,
    They'll put him in the poor-house slick !

"But no, they don't! Not while I own
  The name ov Jedediah ;
Yer movin'? How's yer gran'ma Green,
  An' yer cousin, Ann Maria ?
    Boss, air they? Yas, sirree, I dar
    Tew say, I've got religion thar!"

Preacher, he in his stirrups riz,
  His visage kind ov cheerin';
An' keerful look'd along the road,
  Over sugar bush an' clearin';
    Thar wa'n't a deacon within sight;
    Sez he, "My brother, guess you're right!

"You keep your waggon Zionward,
  With that religion on it;
I calculate we'll meet"—jest here
  A caliker sun bonnet,
    On a sister's head, cum round the Jog,
    An' preacher dispars'd like mornin' fog!

One day a kind ov judgment come,
  The lightnin'-rod conductor
Got broke—the fluid struck his aunt,
  An' in the root-house chuck'd her.
    It laid her up for quite a while,
    An' the judgment made the neighbors smile.

Old Spense he swore a mighty swar,
  He didn't mince nor chew it;
For when he spoke, 'most usual,
  It had a backbone tew it.
    He sed he'd find a healthy plan
    Tew square things with the agent man,

Who'd sold him thet thar useless rod
  To put upon his roofin';
An' ef he found him round the place,

He'd send the scamp a-hoofin'.
"You sort ov understand my sense?"
"Yes, pa," said pooty Deely Spense.

"Yes, pa," sez she, es mild es milk
  Tew thet thar strong oration,
An' when a woman acts like *that*—
  It's bin my observation—
    (An' reckin that you'll find it sound)
    She means tew turn creation round,

An' fix the univarse the way
  She sort ov feels the notion.
So Deely let the old man rave,
  Nor kick'd up no commotion ;
    Tho' thet cute agent man an' she
    Were know'd es steady company.

He'd chance around when Spense was out,
  A feller sort o' airy ;
An' poke around free's the wind,
  With Deely in the dairy.
    (Old Spense hed got a patent churn,
    Thet gev the Church a drefful turn).

I am a married man myself,
  More sot on steddy plowin',
An' cuttin' rails, than praisin' gals,
  Yet honestly allowin'—
    A man must be main hard tew please
    Thet didn't freeze tew Deely's cheese.

OLD SPENSE.

I reckon tho' old Spense hed sign'd
  With Satan queer law papers,
He'd fill'd that dairy up chock-full
  Of them thar patent capers.
    Preacher once took fur sermon text—
    "Rebellious patent vats.—What next?"

I've kind of stray'd from thet thar scare
  That cum on Spense—tho', reely,
I'll allus hold it was a shine
  Of thet thar pooty Deely:
    Thar's them es holds thro' thin an' thick,
    'Twas a friendly visit from Old Nick.

Es time went on, old Spense he seem'd
  More sot on patent capers;
So he went right off tew fetch a thing
  He'd read ov in the papers.
    'Twas a moony night in airly June,
    The Whip-poor-wills wus all in tune;

The Katydids wus callin' clar,
  The fire-bugs wus glowin',
The smell ov clover fill'd the air.
  Thet day old Spense'd bin mowin'—
    With a mower yellin' drefful screams,
    Like them skreeks we hear in nightmare dreams.

Miss Spense wus in the keepin'-room,
  O'erlookin' last yar's cherries;
The Help wus settin' on the bench,

A-hullin' airly berries ;
　The hir'd man sot on the step,
　An' chaw'd, an' watch'd the crickets lep.

Not one ov them thar folks thet thought
　Ov Deely in the dairy :
The Help thought on the hir'd man,
　An' he ov Martin's Mary ;
　　Miss Spense she ponder'd thet she'd found
　　Crush'd sugar'd riz a cent a pound.

I guess hed you an' I bin thar,
　A-peepin' thro' the shutter
Ov thet thar dairy, we'd a swore
　Old Spense's cheese an' butter
　　Wus gilded, from the manner thet
　　Deely she smil'd on pan an' vat.

The Agent he had chanc'd around,
　In evenin's peaceful shadder ;
He'd glimps'd Spense an' his tarrier go
　Across the new-mown medder—
　　To'ard Crampville—so he shew'd his sense,
　　By slidin' o'er the garden fence,

An' kind of unassumin' glode,
　Beneath the bendin' branches,
Tew the dairy door whar Deely watch'd—
　A-twitterin' an' anxious.
　　It didn't suit Miss Deely's plan
　　Her pa should catch that Agent man.

OLD SPENSE.

I kind ov mind them days I went
  With Betsy Ann a-sparking'
Time hed a drefful sneakin' way
  Ov passin' without markin'
    A single blaze upon a post,
    An' walkin' noiseless es a ghost!

I guess thet Adam found it thus,
  Afore he hed to grapple
With thet conundrum Satan rais'd
  About the blam'd old apple;
    He found Time sort ov smart tew pass
    Afore Eve took tew apple sass.

Thar ain't no changes cum about
  Sence them old days in Eden,
Except thet lovers take a spell
  Of mighty hearty feedin'.
    Now Adam makes his Eve rejice
    By orderin' up a lemon ice.

He ain't got enny kind ov show
  To hear the merry pealins'
Of them thar weddin' bells, unless
  He kind ov stirs her feelins'—
    By treatin' her tew ginger pop,
    An' pilin' peanuts in a-top.

Thet Agent man know'd how to run
  The business real handy;
An' him an' Deely sot an' laugh'd,

An' scrunch'd a pile o' candy ;
An' talk'd about the singin' skule—
An' stars—an' Spense's kickin' mule—

An' other elevatin' facts
In Skyence an' in Natur.
An' Time, es I wus sayin', glode
Past, like a champion skater,—
When—Thunder ! round the orchard fence,
Come thet thar tarrier dog an' Spénse,

An' made straight for the dairy door.
Thar's times in most experrence,
We feel how trooly wise 'twould be
To make a rapid clearance ;
Nor wait tew practice them thar rules
We larn tew city dancin' skules.

The Agent es a gen'ral plan
Wus polish'd es the handles
Ov my old plough ; an' slick an' smooth
Es Betsey's tallow candles.
But when he see'd old Spense—wal, neow,
He acted homely es a ceow !

His manners wusn't in the grain,
His wool wus sorter shoddy ;
His courage wus a poorish sort,
It hadn't got no body.
An' when he see'd old Spense, he shook
Es ef he'd see'd his gran'ma's spook.

OLD SPENSE.

Deely she wrung her pooty hands,
  She felt her heart a-turnin'
Es poor es milk when all the cream
  Is taken off fur churnin'.
    When all to once her eyes fell pat
    Upon old Spense's patent vat!

The Agent took no sort ov stock
  Thet time in etiquettin ;
It would hev made a punkin laugh
  Tew see his style of gettin'!
    In thet thar empty vat he slid,
    An' Deely shet the hefty lid.

Old Spense wus smilin' jest es clar
  Es stars in the big " Dipper";
An' Deely made believe tew hum
  "Old Hundred" gay an' chipper,—
    But thinkin' what a tightsome squeeze
    The vat wus fur the Agent's knees.

Old Spense he sed, "I guess, my gal,
  "Ye've been a sort ov dreamin';
"I see ye haven't set the pans,
  "Nor turn'd the mornin's cream in;
    "Now ain't ye spry? Now, darn my hat!
    "Ef the milk's run inter thet thar vat."

Thar's times one's feelin's swell like bread
  In summer-time a-risin',
An' Deely's heart swole in a way

Wus mightily surprisin'.
  When Spense gripp'd one ov them thar pans
  Ov yaller cream in his big han's!

The moon glode underneath a cloud,
  The breeze sigh'd loud an' airy;
The pans they faintlike glimmer'd on
  The white walls ov the dairy.
    Deely she trembl'd like an ash,
    An' lean'd agin the old cnurn dash.

"Tarnation darksome," growl'd old Spense,
  An' liftin' up the cover—
He turn'd the pan ov cream quite spry
  On Deely's Agent lover.
    Good sakes alive! a curdlin' skreek
    From thet thar Agent man did break!

All drippin' white he ros'd tew view,
  His curly locks a-flowin'
With clotted cream, an' in the dusk,
  His eyes with terror glowin'.
    He made one spring—'tis certain, reely,
    He never sed "Good night" tew Deely.

Old Spense he riz up from the ground,
  An' with a kind ov wonder,
He look'd inter thet patent vat,
  An' simply sed, "By thunder"!
    Then look'd at Deely hard, and sed,
    "The milk will sop clar thro' his hed"!

OLD SPENSE.

    Folks look'd right solemn when they heard
      The hull ov thet thar story,
    An' sed, " It might be plainly seen
      'Twas clar agin the glory
        Of Pruvidence to use a vat
        Thet Satan in had boldly sat"!

    They shook their heads when Spense declar'd
      'Twas Deely's beau in hidin';
    They guess'd they know'd a thing or two,
      An' wasn't so confidin':—
        'Twas the " Devourin' Lion" cum
        Tew ask old Spense tew step down hum"!

    Old Spense he kinder spil'd the thing
      Fur thet thar congregation,
    By holdin' on tew life in spite
      Ov Satan's invitation;
        An' hurts thar feelin's ev'ry Spring,
        Buyin' some pesky patent thing.

    The Agent man slid out next day,
      To peddle round young Hyson;
    And Deely fur a fortnight thought
      Ov drinkin' sum rat-pison;
        Didn't put no papers in her har;
        An' din'd out ov the pickle jar.

    Then at Aunt Hesby's sewin'-bee
      She met a slick young feller,
    With a city partin' tew his har
      An' a city umbereller.
        He see'd her hum thet night, an' he
        Is now her steddy company!

THE ROMAN ROSE-SELLER.

Not from Pæstum come my roses; Patrons, see
My flowers are Roman-blown; their nectaries
Drop honey amber, and their petals throw
Rich crimsons on the lucent marble of the shrine
Where snowy Dian lifts her pallid brow,
As crimson lips of Love may seek to warm
A sister glow in hearts as pulseless hewn.
Cæsar from Afric wars returns to-day;
Patricians, buy my royal roses; strew
His way knee-deep, as though old Tiber roll'd
A tide of musky roses from his bed to do
A wonder, wond'rous homage. Marcus Lucius, thou
To-day dost wed; buy roses, roses, roses,
To mingle with the nuptial myrtle; look,
I strip the polish'd thorns from the stems,
The nuptial rose should be a stingless flower;
Lucania, pass not by my roses. Virginia,
Here is a rose that has a canker in't, and yet
It is most glorious-dyed and sweeter smells
Than those death hath not touched. To-day they bear
The shield of Claudius with his spear upon it,
Close upon Cæsar's chariot—heap, heap it up

With roses such as these; 'tis true he's dead
And there's the canker! but, Romans, he
Died glorious, there's the perfume! and his virtues
Are these bright petals; so buy my roses, Widow.
No Greek-born roses mine. Priestess, priestess!
Thy ivory chariot stay; here's a rose and not
A white one, though thy chaste hands attend
On Vesta's flame. Love's of a colour—be it that
Which ladders Heaven and lives amongst the Gods;
Or like the Daffodil blows all about the earth;
Or, Hesperus-like, is one sole star upon
The solemn sky which bridges some sad life,
So here's a crimson rose: Be thou as pure
As Dian's tears iced on her silver cheek,
And know no quality of love, thou art
A sorrow to the Gods! Oh mighty Love!
I would my roses could but chorus Thee.
No roses of Persepolis are mine. Helot, here—
I give thee this last blossom: A bee as red
As Hybla's golden toilers sucked its sweets;
A butterfly, wing'd like to Eros, nipp'd
Its new-pinked leaves; the sun, bright despot, stole
The dew night gives to all. Poor slave, methinks
A bough of cypress were as gay a gift, and yet
It hath some beauty left! a little scarlet—for
The Gods love all; a litte perfume, for there is no life,
Poor slave, but hath its sweetness. Thus I make
My roses Oracles. O hark! the cymbals beat
In god-like silver bursts of sound; I go
To see great Cæsar leading Glory home,
From Campus Martius to the Capitol!

THE WOOING OF GHEEZIS.

The red chief Gheezis, chief of the golden wampum, lay
And watched the west-wind blow adrift the clouds,
With breath all flowery, that from his calumet
Curl'd like to smoke about the mountain tops.
Gheezis look'd from his wigwam, blue as little pools
Drained from the restless mother-wave, that lay
Dreaming in golden hollows of her sands;
And deck'd his yellow locks with feath'ry clouds,
And took his pointed arrows and so stoop'd
And leaning with his red hands on the hills,
Look'd with long glances all along the earth.
" Mudjekeewis, West-Wind, in amongst the forest,
" I see a maid, gold-hued as maize full ripe; her eyes
" Laugh under the dusk boughs like watercourses;
" Her moccasins are wrought with threads of light : her
    hands
" Are full of blue eggs of the robin, and of buds
" Of lilies, and green spears of rice : O Mudjekeewis,
" Who is the maid, gold-hued as maize full-ripen'd?"
" O sun, O Gheezis, that is Spring, is Segwun—woo her!"
" I cannot, for she hides behind the behmagut—
" The thick-leav'd grape-vine, and there laughs upon me."
" O Gheezis," cried Segwun from behind the grape-vine.
" Thy arms are long but all too short to reach me,
" Thou art in heaven and I upon the earth!"
Gheezis, with long golden fingers tore the grape-vine,

But Segwun laughed upon him from behind
A maple, shaking little leaves of gold fresh-budded.
"Gheezis, where are thy feet, O sun, O chief?"
"Follow," sigh'd Mudjekeewis, "Gheezis must wed
"With Spring, with Segwun, or all nature die."
The red chief Gheezis swift ran down the hills,
And as he ran the pools and watercourses
Snatch'd at his yellow hair; the thickets caught
Its tendrils on their brambles; and the buds
That Segwun dropp'd, opened as they touched.
His moccasins were flame, his wampum gold;
His plumes were clouds white as the snow, and red
As Sumach in the moon of falling leaves.
He slipp'd beside the maple, Segwun laugh'd.
"O Gheezis, I am hid amid the lily-pads,
"And thou hast no canoe to seek me there; farewell!"
"I see thine eyes, O Segwun, laugh behind the buds;
"The Manitou is love, and gives me love, and love
"Gives all of power." His moccasins wide laid
Red tracks upon the waves: When Segwun leap'd
Gold-red and laughing from the lily-pads,
To flit before him like a fire-fly, she found
The golden arms of Gheezis round her cast, the buds
Burst into flower in her hands, and all the earth
Laughing where Gheezis look'd; and Mudjekeewis,
Heart-friend of Gheezis, laugh'd, "Now life is come
"Since Segwun and red Gheezis wed and reign!"

BABY'S DREAMS.

What doth the moon so lily white,
Busily weave this Summer night?
Silver ropes and diamond strands
For Baby's pink and dimpl'd hands;
Cords for her rosy palms to hold,
    While she floats, she flies,
To Dream Land set with its shores of gold,
And its buds like stars shaken out of the skies;
Where the trees have tongues and the flowers have lips
    To coax, to kiss,
The velvet cheek of the Babe who slips
Thro' the Dream gate up to a land like this.

What is the mild sea whisp'ring clear
In the rosy shell of Baby's ear?
See! she laughs in her dimpl'd sleep—
What does she hear from the shining deep?

"Thy father comes a-sailing, a-sailing, a-sailing,
Safely comes a-sailing from islands fair and far.
O Baby, bid thy mother cease her tears and bitter wailing
The sailor's wife's his only port, his babe his beacon
    star!"

BABY'S DREAMS.

Softly the Wind doth blow,
What say its murmurs low?
What doth it bring
On the wide soft plume of its dewy wing?
"Only scented blisses
Of innocent, sweet kisses,
For such cheeks as this is,
Of Baby in her nest.
From all the dreaming flowers,
A-nodding in their bowers;
Or bright on leafy towers,
Where the fairy monarchs rest."
"But chiefly I bring,
On my fresh sweet mouth,
Her father's kiss,
As he sails out of the south.
He hitherward blew it at break of day,
I lay it, Babe, on thy tender lip;
I'll steal another and hie away,
And kiss it to him on his wave-rock'd ship."

I saw a fairy twine
Of star-white Jessamine;
A dainty seat shaped like an airy swing;
With two round yellow stars,
Against the misty bars
Of Night; she nailed it high
In the pansy-purple sky,
With four taps of her little rainbow wing.
To and fro
That swing I'll blow.

The baby moon in the amethyst sky
Will laugh at us as we float and fly,
And stretch her silver arms and try
To catch the earth-babe swinging by.

MARY'S TRYST.

Young Mary stole along the vale,
   To keep her tryst with Ulnor's lord;
A warrior clad in coat of mail
   Stood darkling by the brawling ford.

"O let me pass, O let me pass,
   Dark falls the night on hill and lea;
Flies, flies the bright day swift and fast,
   From lordly bow'er and greenwood tree.
The small birds twitter as they fly
   To dewy bough and leaf-hid nest;
Dark fold the black clouds on the sky,
   And maiden terrors throng my breast!"

"And thou shalt pass, thou bonnie maid,
   If thou wilt only tell to me—
Why hiest thou forth in lonesome shade;
   Where may thy wish'd-for bourne be?"

"O let me by, O let me by,
  My granddam dwells by Ulnor's shore;
She strains for me her failing eye—
  Beside her lowly ivied door."

"I rode by Ulnor's shore at dawn,
  I saw no ancient dame and cot;
I saw but startl'd doe and fawn—
  Thy bourne thou yet hast told me not."
"O let me pass—my father lies
  Long-stretch'd in coffin and in shroud,—
Where Ulnor's turrets climb the skies,
  Where Ulnor's battlements are proud!"

"I rode by Ulnor's walls at noon;
  I heard no bell for passing sprite;
And saw no henchman straik'd for tomb;
  Thou hast not told thy bourne aright."
"O let me pass—a monk doth dwell
  In lowly hut by Ulnor's shrine;
I seek the holy friar's cell,
  That he may shrive this soul of mine."

I rode by Ulnor's shrine this day,
  I saw no hut—no friar's cowl;
I heard no holy hermit pray—
  I heard but hooting of the owl!"
"O let me pass—time flies apace—
  And since thou wilt not let me be;
I tryst with chief of Ulnor's race,
  Beneath the spreading hawthorn tree!"

"I rode beside the bonnie thorn,
   When this day's sun was sinking low ;
I saw a damsel like the morn,
   I saw a knight with hound and bow ;
The chief was chief of Ulnor's name,
   The maid was of a high degree ;
I saw him kiss the lovely dame,
   I saw him bend the suitor's knee !

" I saw the fond glance of his eye
   To her red cheek red roses bring ;
Between them, as my steed flew by,
   I saw them break a golden ring."
" O wouldst thou know, thou curious knight,
   Where Mary's bourne to-night will be ?
Since thou has seen such traitor sight,
   Beneath the blooming hawthorn tree."

Fair shone the yellow of her locks,
   Her cheek and bosom's drifted snow ;
She leap'd adown the sharp grey rocks,
   She sought the sullen pool below.
The knight his iron vizard rais'd,
   He caught young Mary to his heart ;
She lifted up her head and gaz'd—
   She drew her yellow locks apart.

The roses touch'd her lovely face ;
   The lilies white did faint and flee ;
The knight was chief of Ulnor's race,—
   His only true love still was she !

"IN EXCHANGE FOR HIS SOUL!"

Long time one whisper'd in his ear—
   "Give me thy strong, pure soul; behold
'Tis mine to give what men hold dear—
   The treasure of red gold."

"I bribe thee not with crown and throne,
   Pale spectres they of kingly pow'r!
I give thee gold—red gold alone
   Can crown a king each hour!"

He frown'd, perchance he felt a throe,
   Gold-hunger gnawing at his heart—
A passing pang—for, stern and low,
   He bade the fiend depart!

Again there came the voice and said:
   "Gold for that soul of thine were shame;
Thine be that thing for which have bled
   Both Gods and men,—high Fame.

"And in long ages yet to sweep
   Their gloom and glory on the day;
When mould'ring kings, forgot, shall sleep
   In ashes, dust, and clay:

"Thy name shall, starlike, pulse and burn
   On heights most Godlike; and divine,
Immortal bays thy funereal urn
   Shall lastingly entwine!"

He sigh'd ; perchance he felt the thrill,
  The answ'ring pulse to Fame's high call ;
But answer made his steadfast will—
  " I will not be thy thrall !"

Again there came the voice and cried :
  " Dost thou my kingly bribes disdain ?
Yet shalt thou barter soul and pride
  For things ignobly vain !

" Two shameless eyes—two false, sweet eyes—
  A sinful brow of sinless white,
Shall hurl thy soul from high clear skies
  To ME, and Stygian night.

" Beneath the spell of gilded hair,
  Thy palms, like sickly weeds, shall die !
God-strong Resolves, a sensuous air
  Shall mock and crucify.

" Go to ! my thrall at last thou art !
  Ere bud to rounded blossom change ;
Thou wilt for wanton lips and heart
  Most false, thy soul exchange !"

THE LAND OF KISSES.

Where is the Land of Kisses,
    Can you tell, tell, tell?
Ah, yes ; I know its blisses
        Very well !
'Tis not beneath the swinging
        Of the Jessamine,
Where gossip-birds sit singing
        In the vine !

Where is the Land of Kisses,
    Do you know, know, know?
Is it such a land as this is ?
        No, truly no !
Nor is it 'neath the Myrtle,
        Where each butterfly
Can brush your lady's kirtle,
        Flitting by !

Where is the Land of Kisses,
    Can you say, say, say?
Yes ; there a red lip presses
        Mine ev'ry day !
But 'tis not where the Pansies
        Open purple eyes,
And gossip all their fancies
        To the skies !

.I know the Land of Kisses
    Passing well, well, well;
Who seeks it often misses—
        Let me tell.
Fly, lover, like a swallow,
        Where your lady goes;
You'll find it if you follow,
        'Neath the Rose.

SAID THE THISTLE-DOWN.

"If thou wilt hold my silver hair,
    O Lady sweet and bright;
I'll bring thee, maiden darling, where
    Thy lover is to-night.
Lay down thy robe of cloth of gold—
    Gold weigheth heavily,
Thy necklace wound in jewell'd fold,
    And hie thee forth with me."

"O Thistle-down, dear Thistle-down,
    I've laid my robe aside;
My necklace and my jewell'd crown,
    And yet I cannot glide
Along the silver crests of night
    With thee, light thing, with thee.
Fain would I try the airy flight,
    What sayest thou to me?"

"If thou wilt hold my silver hair,
  O maiden fair and proud ;
We'll float upon the purple air
  High as yon lilied cloud.
There is a jewel weighs thy heart ;
  If thou with me wouldst glide
That cold, cold jewel place apart—
  The jewel of thy pride ! "

" O Thistle-down, dear Thistle-down—
  That jewel part I've set :
With golden robe and shining crown
  And cannot follow yet !
Fain would I clasp thy silver tress
  And float on high with thee ;
Yet somewhat me to earth doth press—
  What sayest thou to me ?

" If thou wilt hold my silver hair
  O lady, sweet and chaste ;
We'll dance upon the sparkling air
  And to thy lover haste.
A lily lies upon thy breast
  Snow-white as it can be—
It holds thee strong—sweet, with the rest
  Yield lilied chastity."

" O Thistle-down, false Thistle-down
  I've parted Pride and Gold ;
Laid past my jewels and my crown—
  My golden robings' fold.

I will not lay my lily past—
 Love's light as vanity
When to the mocking wind is cast
 The lily, Chastity."

BOUCHE-MIGNONNE.

Bouche-Mignonne liv'd in the mill,
 Past the vineyards shady;
Where the sun shone on a rill
 Jewell'd like a lady.
Proud the stream with lily-bud,
 Gay with glancing swallow;
Swift its trillion-footed flood,
 Winding ways to follow.
Coy and still when flying wheel
 Rested from its labour;
Singing when it ground the meal
 Gay as lute or tabor.
"Bouche-Mignonne" it called, when, red
 In the dawn were glowing,
Eaves and mill-wheel, "leave thy bed,
 "Hark to me a-flowing!"

Bouche-Mignonne awoke and quick
    Glossy tresses braided;
Curious sunbeams cluster'd thick
    Vines her casement shaded.
Deep with leaves and blossoms white
    Of the morning-glory,
Shaking all their banners bright
    From the mill eaves hoary.
Swallows turn'd glossy throats,
    Timorous, uncertain,
When to hear their matin notes,
    Peep'd she thro' her curtain,
Shook the mill-stream sweet and clear,
    With its silver laughter—
Shook the mill from flooring sere
    Up to oaken rafter.
"Bouche-Mignonne" it cried "come down!
    "Other flowers are stirring;
"Pierre with fingers strong and brown
    "Sets the wheel a-birring."

Bouche-Mignonne her distaff plies
    Where the willows shiver,
Round the mossy mill-wheel flies;
    Dragon-flies a-quiver—
Flash a-thwart the lily-beds
    Pierce the dry reed's thicket:
Where the yellow sunlight treads
    Chants the friendly cricket.
Butterflies about her skim
    (Pouf! their simple fancies!)
In the willow shadows dim

Take her eyes for pansies!
Buzzing comes a velvet bee
  Sagely it supposes
Those red lips beneath the tree
  Are two crimson roses!
Laughs the mill-stream wise and bright
  It is not so simple
Knew it, since she first saw light
  Ev'ry blush and dimple!
" Bouche-Mignonne " it laughing cries
  " Pierre as the bee is silly
" Thinks two morning stars thine eyes—
  " And thy neck a lily!"

Bouche-Mignonne when shadows crept
  From the vine-dark hollows;
When the mossy mill-wheel slept
  Curv'd the airy swallows.
When the lilies clos'd white lids
  Over golden fancies—
Homeward drove her goats and kids,
  Bright the gay moon dances.
With her light and silver feet,
  On the mill-stream flowing,
Come a thousand perfumes sweet,
  Dewy buds are blowing.
Comes an owl and grely flits
  Jewell'd ey'd and hooting—
Past the green tree where she sits
  Nightingales are fluting
Soft the wind as rust'ling silk
  On a courtly lady,

Tinkles down the flowing milk
    Huge and still and shady—
Stands the mill-wheel resting still
    From its loving labor,
Dances on the tireless rill
    Gay as lute or tabor !
" Bouche-Mignonne " it laughing cries
    " Do not blush and tremble ;
" If the night has ears and eyes
    " I'll for thee disemble !
" Loud and clear and sweet I'll sing
    " Oh my far way straying,
" I will hide the whisper'd thing
    " Pierre to thee is saying.
" Bouche-Mignonne, good night, good night !
    " Ev'ry silver hour
" I will toss my lilies white
    "'Gainst thy maiden bower !"

BESIDE THE SEA.

One time he dream'd beside a sea,
    That laid a mane of mimic stars ;
In fondling quiet on the knee,
    Of one tall, pearl'd, cliff—the bars ;
Of golden beaches upward swept,
    Pine-scented shadows seaward crept.

The full moon swung her ripen'd sphere
  As from a vine; and clouds as small
As vine leaves in the opening year
  Kissed the large circle of her ball.
The stars gleamed thro' them as one sees
Thro' vine leaves drift the golden bees.

He dream'd beside this purple sea,
  Low sang its trancèd voice, and he—
He knew not if the wordless strain
  Made prophecy of joy or pain;
He only knew far stretch'd that sea,
He knew its name—Eternity!

A shallop with a rainbow sail,
  On the bright pulses of the tide,
Throbb'd airily; a fluting gale
  Kiss'd the rich gilding of its side;
By chain of rose and myrtle fast,
A light sail touch'd the slender mast.

" A flower-bright rainbow thing," he said
  To one beside him, " far too frail
" To brave dark storms that lurk ahead,
  " To dare sharp talons of the gale.
" Belov'd, thou woulds't not forth with me
" In such a bark on such a sea?"

" First tell me of its name?" she bent
  Her eyes divine and innocent
On his. He raised his hand above
  Its prow, and answ'ring swore, " 'Tis Love!"

"Now tell," she ask'd, "how is it built,
Of gold or worthless timber gilt?"

"Of gold," he said. "Whence named?" asked
   The roses of her lips apart,   [she,
She paus'd—a lily by the sea—
   Came his swift answer, "From my heart!"
She laid her light palm in his hand.
"Let loose the shallop from the strand!"

THE HIDDEN ROOM.

   I marvel if my heart,
   Hath any room apart,
Built secretly its mystic walls within;
   With subtly warded key
   Ne'er yielded unto me—
Where even I have surely never been.

   Ah, surely I know all
   The bright and cheerful hall
With the fire ever red upon its hearth;
   My friends dwell with me there,
   Nor comes the step of Care
To sadden down its music and its mirth.

THE HIDDEN ROOM.

    Full well I know as mine,
    The little cloister'd shrine
No foot but mine alone hath ever trod;
    There come the shining wings—
    The face of one who brings
The pray'rs of men before the throne of God.

    And many know full well,
    The busy, busy cell,
Where I toil at the work I have to do,
    Nor is the portal fast,
    Where stand phantoms of the past,
Or grow the bitter plants of darksome rue.

    I know the dainty spot
    (Ah, who doth know it not?)
Where pure young Love his lily-cradle made;
    And nestled some sweet springs
    With lily-spangled wings—
Forget-me-nots upon his bier I laid.

    Yet marvel I, my soul,
    Know I thy very whole,
Or dost thou hide a chamber still from me?
    Is it built upon the wall?
    Is it spacious? is it small?
Is it God, or man, or I who holds the key?

FARMER DOWNS CHANGES HIS OPINION OF NATURE.

"No," said old Farmer Downs to me,
  "I ain't the facts denyin',
That all young folks in love must be,
  As birds must be a-flyin'.
Don't go agin sech facts, because
I'm one as re-specks Natur's laws.

"No, sir! Old Natur knows a thing
  Or two, I'm calculatin',
She don't make cat-fish dance and sing,
  Or sparrow-hawks go skatin';
She knows her business ev'ry time,
You bet your last an' lonely dime!

"I guess, I'm posted pooty fair
  On that old gal's capers;
She allers acts upon the square
  Spite o' skyentific papers.
(I borrows one most ev'ry week
From Jonses down to "Pincher's Creek.")

"It sorter freshens up a man
   To read the newest notions,
Tho' I don't freeze much tew that thar plan,
   About the crops ratotions;
You jest leave Natur do her work,
   She'll do it! she ain't one tew shirk!

"I'm all fur lettin Natur go
   The way she's sot on choosin'.
Ain't that the figger of a beau
   That's talkin' thar tew Susan?
Down by the orchard snake-fence? Yes.
All right, it's Squire Sims, I guess.

"He's jest the one I want tew see
   Come sparkin'; guess they're lyin',
That say that of old age he be
   Most sartinly a-dyin'—
He's no sech thing! Good sakes alive,
The man is only seventy-five!

"An' she's sixteen. I'm not the man
   Tew act sort of inhuman,
An' meanly spile old Natur's plan
   To jine a man and woman
In wedlock's bonds. Sirree, she makes,
This grand old Natur, no mistakes.

"They're standin' pooty clus; the leaves
   Is round 'em like a bower,
The Squire's like the yaller sheaves

An' she's the Corn Flower,
Natur's the binder, allus true,
Tew make one heart of them thar two.

"Yas—as I was a-sayin', friend,
  I'm all for Natur's teachins;
She ain't one in the bitter end
  Tew practice over-reachins.
You trust her, and she'll treat you well,
Don't doubt her by the leastest spell.

"I'm not quite clar but subsoil looks
  Jest kinder not quite pious;
I sorter think them farmin' books,
  Will in the long run sky us,
Right in the mud; the way they balk
Old Natur with thar darn fool talk!

"When Susie marries Squire Sims,
  I'll lease his upland farm;
I'll get it cheap enough from him—
  Jest see his long right arm
About her waist—looks orful big!
Why, gosh! he's bought a new brown wig!

"Wal, that's the way old Natur acts
  When bald folks go a-sparkin';
The skyentists can't alter facts
  With all their hard work larkin',
A sparkin man *will* look his best—
That's Na'ur—tain't no silly jest!

"Old Natur, you and me is twins;
   I never will git snarly
With you, old gal. Why, darn my shins!
   That's only Jonses Charlie.
She's cuddlin' right agin his vest!
Eh? What? 'Old Natur knows what's best!'"

"Oh, does she? Wal, p'raps 'tis so;
   Jest see the rascal's arm
About her waist! You've got tew go
   Young man, right off this farm;
Old Natur knows a pile, no doubt,
But you an' her hed best get out!

"You, Susie, git right hum. I'm mad
   Es enny bilin' crater!
In futur, sick or well or sad
   I'll take no stock in Natur.
I'm that disgusted with her capers
I'll run the farm by skyence papers."

THE BURGOMEISTER'S WELL.

A peaceful spot, a little street,
   So still between the double roar
Of sea and city that it seemed
   A rest in music, set before

Some clashing chords—vibrating yet
   With hurried measures fast and sweet ;
For so the harsh chords of the town,
   And so the ocean's rythmic beat.

A little street with linden trees
   So thickly set, the belfry's face
Was leaf-veiled, while above them pierced
   Four slender spires flamboyant grace,
Old porches carven when the trees,
   Were seedlings yellow in the sun
Five hundred years ago that bright
   Upon the quaint old city shone.

A fountain prim, and richly cut
   In ruddy granite, carved to tell
How a good burgomeister rear'd
   The stone above the people's well.
A sea-horse from his nostrils blew
   Two silver threads ; a dragon's lip
Dropp'd di'monds, and a giant hand
   Held high an urn on finger tip.

'Twas there I met my little maid,
   There saw her flaxen tresses first ;
She filled the cup for one who lean'd
   (A soldier, crippl'd and athirst)
Against the basin's carven rim ;
   Her dear small hand's white loveliness
Was pinkly flush'd, the gay bright drops
   Plash'd on her brow and silken dress.

I took the flagon from her hand,
    Too small, dear hand, for such a weight.
From cobweb weft and woof is spun
    The tapestry of Life and Fate !
The linden trees had gilded buds,
    The dove wheeled high on joyous wing,
When on that darling hand of hers
    I slipped the glimmer of a ring.
Ah, golden heart and golden locks
    Ye wove so sweet, so sure a spell !
That quiet day I saw her first
    Beside the Burgomeister's Well !

SAID THE WIND.

"Come with me," said the Wind
To the ship within the dock.
" Or dost thou fear the shock
Of the ocean-hidden rock,
When tempests strike thee full and leave thee blind ;
And low the inky clouds,
Blackly tangle in thy shrouds ;
And ev'ry strainèd cord
Finds a voice and shrills a word,
That word of doom so thunderously upflung
    From the tongue

　　　　Of every forkèd wave,
　　　　Lamenting o'er a grave
　　　　Deep hidden at its base,
　　Where the dead whom it has slain
　　　　Lie in the strict embrace
　　Of secret weird tendrils ; but the pain
　　　　Of the ocean's strong remorse
　　　　Doth fiercely force
　　The tale of murder from its bosom out
　　In a mighty tempest clangour, and its shout
　　In the threat'ning and lamenting of its swell
　　　　Is as the voice of Hell,
　　Yet all the word it saith
　　　　Is ' Death.' "

　　　　" Come with me," sang the Wind,
　　　　Why art thou, love, unkind ?
　　　　Thou are too fair, O ship,
　　　　To kiss the slimy lip
　　Of the cold and dismal shore ; and, prithee, mark,
　　　　How chill and dark
　　Shew the vast and rusty linkings of the chain,
　　　　Hoarse grating as with pain,
　　　　Which moors thee
　　　　And secures thee
　　From the transports of the soft wind and the main.
　　　　Aye ! strain thou and pull,
　　　　Thy sails are dull
　　And dim from long close furling on thy spars,
　　　　But come thou forth with me,
　　　　And full and free,

I'll kiss them, kiss them, kiss them, till they be
 White as the Arctic stars,
Or as the salt-white pinions of the gull!"

"Come with me," sang the Wind,
 "O ship belov'd, and find
 How golden-gloss'd and blue
 Is the sea,
How thrush-sweet is my voice; how dearly true
 I'll keep my nuptial promises to thee.
 O mine to guide thy sails
 By the kisses of my mouth;
 Soft as blow the gales,
 On the roses in the south.
 O mine to guide thee far
 From ruddy coral bar,
From horizon to horizon thou shalt glimmer like a star;
 Thou shalt lean upon my breast,
 And I shall rest,
 And murmur in thy sails,
 Such fond tales,
 That thy finest cords
 Will, syren-like, chant back my mellow words
 With such renew'd enchantment unto me
 That I shall be,
By my own singing, closer bound to thee!"

"Come with me," sang the Wind,
 "Thou knowest, love, my mind,
 No more I'll try to woo thee,
 Persuade thee or pursue thee,

For thou art mine;
Since first thy mast, a tall and stately pine
    Beneath Norwegian skies,
    Sang to my sighs.
    Thou, thou wert built for me,
    Strong lily of the sea!
    Thou cans't not choose,
The calling of my low voice to refuse;
    And if Death
Were the sole, sad, wailing burthen of my breath,
    Thy timbers at my call,
    Would shudder in their thrall,
Thy sails outburst to touch my stormy lip;
    Like a giant quick in a grave,
    Thy anchor heave,
And close upon my thunder-pulsing breast, O ship,
    Thou would'st tremble, nor repine,
    That being mine,
    Thy spars,
Like long pale lights of falling stars,
Plunged in the Stygian blackness of the sea,
    And to billowy ruin cast
    Thy tall and taper mast,
Rushed shrieking headlong down to an abyss.
    O ship! O love! if Death
Were such sure portion, thou could'st not refuse
    But thou would'st choose
As mine to die, and call such choosing bliss;
    For thou for me
Wert plann'd from all eternity!"

THE GHOSTS OF THE TREES.

The silver fangs of the mighty axe,
  Bit to the blood of our giant boles ;
It smote our breasts aud smote our backs,
  Thunder'd the front-cleared leaves—
    As sped in fire,
The whirl and flame of scarlet leaves,
  With strong desire .
Leaped to the air our captive souls.

While down our corpses thunder'd,
The air at our strong souls gazed and wondered ;
  And cried to us, " Ye
Are full of all mystery to me !
  I saw but thy plumes of leaves,
    Thy strong, brown greaves ;
Thy sinewy roots and lusty branches,
And fond and anxious,
  I laid my ear and my restless breast
    By each pride-high crest ;
    And softly stole
And listen'd by limb and listen'd by bole,
Nor ever the stir of a soul,
    Heard I in ye—
  Great is the mystery ! "

The strong, brown eagle plung'd from his peak,
From the hollow iron of his beak ;

The wood pigeon fell ; its breast of blue
Cold with sharp death all thro' and thro',
    To our ghosts he cried.
  " With talons of steel,
    I hold the storm ;
  Where the high peaks reel,
    My young lie warm.
In the wind-rock'd spaces of air I bide ;
  My wings too wide—
Too angry-strong for the emerald gyves,
Of woodland cell where the meek dove thrives.
  And when at the bar,
Of morn I smote with my breast its star,
    And under—
My wings grew purple, the jealous thunder,
  With the flame of the skies
Hot in my breast, and red in my eyes ;
  From peak to peak of sunrise pil'd
That set space glowing,
With flames from air-based crater's blowing—
  I downward swept, beguiled
By the close-set forest gilded and spread
A sea for the lordly tread,
  Of a God's war-ship —
I broke its leafy turf with my breast ;
    My iron lip
I dipp'd in the cool of each whispering crest ;
  From thy leafy steeps,
  I saw in my deeps,
Red coral the flame necked oriole—
But never the stir of a soul

Heard I in ye—
Great is the mystery!"

From its ferny coasts,
The river gazed at our strong, free ghosts,
  And with rocky fingers shed
  Apart the silver curls of its head;
Laid its murmuring hands,
On the reedy bands;
  And at gaze
Stood in the half-moon's of brown, still bays;
Like gloss'd eyes of stags
Its round pools gaz'd from the rusty flags,
  At our ghostly crests
At the bark-shields strong on our phantom breasts;
  And its tide
Took lip and tongue and cried.
  " I have push'd apart
  The mountain's heart;
  I have trod the valley down;
    With strong hands curled,
    Have caught and hurled,
  To the earth the high hill's crown!

  My brow I thrust,
  Through sultry dust,
That the lean wolf howl'd upon;
  I drove my tides,
  Between the sides,
Of the bellowing canon.

THE GHOSTS OF THE TREES.

From chrystal shoulders,
I hurled my boulders,
On the bridge's iron span.
When I rear'd my head
From its old time bed,
Shook the pale cities of man !

I have run a course
With the swift, wild horse ;
I have thunder'd pace for pace,
With the rushing herds—
I have caught the beards
Of the swift stars in the race !

Neither moon nor sun
Could me out-run ;
Deep cag'd in my silver bars,
I hurried with me,
To the shouting sea,
Their light and the light of the stars !

The reeling earth
In furious mirth
With sledges of ice I smote.
I whirled my sword,
Where the pale berg roar'd,
I took the ship by the throat !

With stagnant breath
I called chill Death
My guest to the hot bayou.

I built men's graves,
With strong thew'd waves
That thing that my strength might do.

I did right well—
Men cried " From Hell
The might of Thy hand is given !"
By loose rocks stoned
The stout quays groaned,
Sleek sands by my spear were riven.

O'er shining slides,
On my gloss'd tides,
The brown cribs close woven roll'd ;
The stout logs sprung,
Their height among
My loud whirls of white and gold !

The great raft prest,
My calm, broad breast—
A dream thro' my shady trance,
The light canoe—
A spirit flew—
The pulse of my blue expanse.

Wing'd swift the ships,
My foaming lips
Made rich with dewy kisses,
All night and morn,
Field's red with corn,
And where the mill-wheel hisses.

And shivers and sobs,
With lab'ring throbs,
With its whirls my strong palms play'd.
I parted my flags,
For thirsty stags,
On the necks of arches laid.

To the dry-vined town
My tide roll'd down—
Dry lips and throats a-quiver,
Rent sky and sod
With shouts ".From God
The strength of the mighty river!"

I, list'ning, heard
The soft-song'd bird;
The beetle about thy boles.
The calling breeze
In thy crests, O Trees—
Never the voices of souls!"

We, freed souls, of the Trees look'd down
On the river's shining eyes of brown;
And upward smiled
At the tender air and its warrior child,
The iron eagle strong and wild.

" No will of ours,
The captive souls of our barky tow'rs;
" His the deed
Who laid in the secret earth the seed;

And with strong hand
Knitted each woody fetter and band.
  Never, ye
Ask of the tree,
The " Wherefore " or " Why " the tall trees stand,
Built in their places on the land !
  Their souls unknit ;
With any wisdom or any wit,
  The subtle " Why, "
Ask ye not of earth or sky—
  But one command it.

GISLI : THE CHIEFTAIN.

To the Goddess Lada prayed
  Gisli, holding high his spear
Bound with buds of spring, and laughed
  All his heart to Lada's ear.

Damp his yellow beard with mead,
  Loud the harps clang'd thro the day;
With bruised breasts triumphant rode
  Gisli's galleys in the bay.

Bards sang in the banquet hall,
  Set in loud verse Gisli's fame,
On their lips the war gods laid
  Fire to chaunt their warrior's name.

To the Love-queen Gisli pray'd,
　Buds upon his tall spear's tip;
Laughter in his broad blue eyes,
　Laughter on his bearded lip.

To the Spring-queen Gisli pray'd,
　She, with mystic distaff slim,
Spun her hours of love and leaves,
　Made the stony headlands dim—

Dim and green with tender grass,
　Blew on ice-fields with red mouth;
Blew on lovers hearts; and lured
　White swans from the blue-arched south.

To the Love-queen Gisli pray'd,
　Groan'd far icebergs tall and blue
As to Lada's distaff slim,
　All their ice-locked fires flew.

To the Love-queen Gisli prayed,
　She, with red hands, caught and spun
Yellow flames from crater lips,
　Long flames from the waking sun.

To the Love-queen Gisli prayed,
　She with loom and beam and spell,
All the subtle fires of earth
　Wove, and wove them strong and well.

To the Spring-queen Gisli prayed,
　Low the sun the pale sky trod;
Mute her ruddy hand she raised
　Beckon'd back the parting God.

To the Love-queen Gisli prayed—
  Weft and woof of flame she wove—
Lada, Goddess of the Spring!
  Lada, Goddess strong of Love!

Sire of the strong chieftain's prayer,
  Victory with his pulse of flame;
Mead its mother—loud he laughed,
  Calling on great Lada's name.

" Goddess Lada--Queen of Love!
  " Here stand I and quaff to thee—
" Deck for thee with buds my spear—
  " Give a comely wife to me!

" Blow not to my arms a flake
  " Of crisp snow in maiden guise;
" Mists of pallid hair and tips
  " Of long ice-spears in her eyes!

" When my death-sail skims the foam—
  " Strain my oars on Death's black sea—
" When my foot the " Glass-Hill " seeks—
  " Such a maid may do for me!

" Now, O Lada, mate the flesh!
  " Mate the fire and flame of life,
" Tho' the soul go still unwed,
  " Give the flesh its fitting wife!

" As the galley runs between,
  " Skies with billows closely spun;
" Feeling but the wave that leaps
  " Closest to it in the sun "

"Throbs but to the present kiss
  "Of the wild lips of the sea ;
Thus a man joys in his life—
  Nought of the Beyond knows he !

"Goddess ! here I cast bright buds,
  "Spicy pine boughs at thy feet ;
"Give the flesh its fitting mate
  "Life is strong and life is sweet !

To the Love-queen Gisli pray'd—
  Weft and woof of flame she wove :
Lada, Goddess of the Spring—
  Lada, Goddess strong of Love !

Part II.

From harpings and sagas and mirth of the town,
Great Gisli, the chieftain strode merrily down.

His ruddy beard stretch'd in the loom of the wind,
His shade like a dusky-God striding behind.

Gylfag, his true hound, to his heel glided near,
Sharp-fang'd, lank and red as a blood-rusted spear.

As crests of the green bergs flame white in the sky,
The town on its sharp hill shone brightly and high.

In fiords roared the ice below the dumb stroke
Of the Sun's red hammer rose blue mist like smoke.

It clung to the black pines, and clung to the bay—
The galleys of Gisli grew ghosts of the day.

It followed the sharp wings of swans, as they rose—
It fell to the wide jaws of swift riven floes.

It tam'd the wild shriek of the eagle—grew dull
The cries, in its foldings, of osprey and gull.

" Arouse thee, bold wind," shouted Gisli " and drive
" Floe and Berg out to sea as bees from a hive.

" Chase this woman-lipped haze at top of thy speed,
" It cloys to the soul as the tongue cloys with mead !

" Come, buckle thy sharp spear again to thy breast !
" Thy galley hurl forth from the seas of the West.

" With thy long, hissing oars, beat loud the north sea.
" The sharp gaze of day give the eagles and me.

" No cunning mists shrouding the sea and the sky,
" Or the brows of the great Gods, bold wind, love I !

" As Gylfag, my hound, lays his fangs in the flank
" Of a grey wolf, shadowy, leather-thew'd, lank.

" Bold wind, chase the blue mist, thy prow in its hair,
" Sun, speed thy keen shafts thro' the breast of the air !

Part III.

The shouting of Gisli, the chieftain,
Rock'd the blue hazes, and cloven

In twain by sharp prow of the west wind,
To north and to south fled the thick mist.

As in burnish'd walls of Valhalla,
In cleft of the mist stood the chieftain,
And up to the blue shield of Heaven,
Flung the loud shaft of his laughter.

Smote the mist, with shrill spear the swift wind,
Grey shapes fled like ghosts on the Hell way;
Bay'd after their long locks hoarse Gylfag,
Stared at them, triumphant, the eagles.

To mate and to eaglets, the eagle
Shriek'd, "Gone is my foe of the deep mist,
" Rent by the vast hands of the kind Gods,
" Who knows the knife-pangs of our hunger!"

Shrill whistled the winds as his dun wings
Strove with it feather by feather;
Loud grated the rock as his talons
Its breast spurned slowly his red eyes.

Like fires seemed to flame in the swift wind,
At his sides the darts of his hunger—
At his ears the shriek of his eaglets—
In his breast the love of the quarry.

Unfurl'd to the northward and southward
His wings broke the air, and to eastward
His breast gave its iron; and God-ward
Pierc'd the shrill voice of his hunger.

Bared were his great sides as he laboured
Up the first steep blue of the broad sky ;
His gaze on the fields of his freedom,
To the God's spoke the prayers of his gyres.

Bared were his vast sides as he glided
Black in the sharp blue of the north sky ;
Black over the white of the tall cliffs,
Black over the arrow of Gisli.

THE SONG OF THE ARROW.

What know I,
As I bite the blue veins of the throbbing sky ;
To the quarry's breast,
Hot from the sides of the sleek smooth nest ?

What know I
Of the will of the tense bow from which I fly !
What the need or jest,
That feathers my flight to its bloody rest.

What know I
Of the will of the bow that speeds me on high ?
What doth the shrill bow
Of the hand on its singing soul-string know ?

Flame-swift speed I—
And the dove and the eagle shriek out and die ;
Whence comes my sharp zest
For the heart of the quarry ? the Gods know best.

Deep pierc'd the red gaze of the eagle—
The breast of a cyguet below him ;
Beneath his dun wing from the eastward
Shrill-chaunted the long shaft of Gisli !

Beneath his dun wing from the westward
Shook a shaft that laugh'd in its biting—
Met in the fierce breast of the eagle
The arrows of Gisli and Brynhild !

Part IV.

A ghost along the Hell-way sped,
The Hell-shoes shod his misty tread ;
A phantom hound beside him sped.

Beneath the spandrils of the Way,
World's roll'd to-night—from night to day ;
In space's ocean Suns were spray.

Group'd world's, eternal eagles, flew ;
Swift comets fell like noiseless dew,
Young earths slow budded in the blue.

The waves of space inscrutable,
With awful pulses rose and fell—
Silent and godly—terrible.

Electric souls of strong Suns laid,
Strong hands along the awful shade
That God about His God-work made.

Ever from all ripe worlds did break,
Men's voices, as when children speak.
Eager and querulous and weak.

And pierc'd to the All-worker thro'
His will that veil'd Him from the view
" What hast thou done ? What dost thou do ?

And ever from His heart did flow
Majestical, the answer low—
The benison " Ye shall not know !

The wan ghost on the Hell-way sped,
Nor yet Valhalla's lights were shed
Upon the white brow of the Dead.

Nor sang within his ears the roll
Of trumpets calling to his soul ;
Nor shone wide portals of the goal.

His spear grew heavy on his breast,
Dropp'd, like a star his golden crest ;
Far, far the vast Halls of the Blest !

His heart grown faint, his feet grown weak,
He scal'd the knit mists of a peak,
That ever parted grey and bleak.

And, as by unseen talons nipp'd,
To deep Abysses slowly slipp'd ;
Then, swift as thick smoke strongly ripp'd.

By whirling winds from ashy ring,
Of dank weeds blackly smoldering,
The peak sprang upward a quivering

And perdurable, set its face
Against the pulsing breast of space
But for a moment to its base.

Refluent roll'd the crest new sprung,
In clouds with ghastly lightnings stung,—
Faint thunders to their black feet clung.

His faithful hound ran at his heel—
His thighs and breast were bright with steel—
He saw the awful Hellway reel.

But far along its bleak peaks rang
A distant trump—its airy clang
Like light through deathly shadows sprang.

He knew the blast—the voice of love!
Cleft lay the throbbing peak above
Sail'd light, wing'd like a silver dove.

On strove the toiling ghost, his soul
Stirr'd like strong mead in wassail bowl,
That quivers to the shout of "Skoal.!"

Strode from the mist close-curv'd and cold
As is a writhing dragon's fold;
A warrior with shield of gold.

A sharp blade glitter'd at his hip,
Flamed like a star his lance's tip;
His bugle sang at bearded lip.

Beneath his golden sandels flew
Stars from the mist as grass flings dew;
Or red fruit falls from the dark yew.

As under shelt'ring wreaths of snow
The dark blue north flowers richly blow—
Beneath long locks of silver glow.

Clear eyes, that burning on a host
Would win a field at sunset lost,
Ere stars from Odin's hand were toss'd.

He stretch'd his hand, he bowed his head;
The wan ghost to his bosom sped—
Dead kiss'd the bearded lips of Dead !

" What dost thou here, my youngest born ?
" Thou—scarce yet fronted with life's storm—
" Why art thou from the dark earth torn ?

" When high Valhalla puls'd and rang
" With harps that shook as grey bards sang—
" 'Mid the loud joy I heard the clang.

" Of Death's dark doors—to me alone
" Smote in thy awful dying groan—
My soul recall'd its blood and bone.

" Viewless the cord which draws from far
" To the round sun some mighty star ;
Viewless the strong-knit soul-cords are ! "

" I felt thy dying gasp—thy soul
" Towards mine a kindred wave in roll,
" I left the harps—I left the bowl."

" I sought the Hellway—I—the blest ;
" That thou, new death-born son should rest
Upon the strong rock of my breast.

GISLI: THE CHIEFTAIN.

What dost thou here, young, fair and bold ?
" Sleek with youth's gloss thy locks of gold ;
Thy years by flow'rs might yet be told !

" What dost thou at the ghostly goal,
" While yet thy years were to thy soul,
" As mead yet shallow in the bowl ? "

His arm about the pale ghost cast,
The warrior blew a clear, loud blast ;
Like frighten'd wolves the mists fled past.

Grew firm the way ; worlds flame to light
The awful peak that thrusts its height,
With swift throbs upward, like a flight.

Of arrows from a host close set
Long meteors pierc'd its breast of jet—
Again the trump his strong lips met—

And at its blast blew all the day,
In broad winds on the awful Way ;
Sun smote at Sun across the grey ;

As reindeer smite the high-pil'd snow
To find the green moss far below—
They struck the mists thro' which did glow

Bright vales—and on a sea afar,
Lay at a sunlit harbour bar,
A galley gold-sail'd like a star !

Spake the pale ghost as onward sped
Heart-press'd to heart the valiant dead ;
Soft the green paths beneath their tread.

" I lov'd, this is my tale, and died—
" The fierce chief hunger'd for my bride—
" The spear of Gisli pierc'd my side !

" And she—her love fill'd all my need—
Her vows were sweet and strong as mead ;
Look, father—doth my heart still bleed ?

" I built her round with shaft and spear,
I kept her mine for one brief year—
She laugh'd above my blood stain'd bier !

" Upon a far and ice-peak'd coast
My galleys by long winds were toss'd—
There Gisli feasted with his host.

" Of warriors triumphant—he
Strode out from harps and revelry ;
And sped his shaft above the sea !

" Look, father, doth my heart bleed yet ?
His arrow Brynhild's arrow met—
My gallies anchor'd in their rest.

" Again their arrows meet—swift lies
That pierc'd me from their smiling eyes ;
How fiercely hard a man's heart dies !

" She false—he false ! There came a day
Pierc'd by the fierce chief's spear I lay—
My ghost rose shrieking from its clay.

I saw on Brynhild's golden vest
The shining locks of Gisli rest;
I sought the Hell-way to the Blest.

"Father, put forth thy hand and tear
Their twin shafts from my heart, all bare
To thee—they rankle death-like there !

Said the voice of Evil to the ear of Good,
  "Clasp thou my strong, right hand,
"Nor shall our clasp be known or understood
  "By any in the land."

"I, the dark giant, rule strongly on the earth,
  "Yet thou, bright one, and I
"Sprang from the one great mystery—at one birth
  "We looked upon the sky !

"I labour at my bleak, my stern toil accurs'd
  "Of all mankind—nor stay,
To rest, to murmur "I hunger" or "I thirst !"
  Nor for my joy delay.

"My strength pleads strongly with thee ; doth any
    beat
  With hammer and with stone
Past tools to use them to his deep defeat—
  To turn them on his throne ?

"Then I of God the mystery—toil thou with me
  Brother ; but in the sight
Of men who know not, I, the stern son shall be
  Of Darkness—Thou of Light !"

THE SHELL.

O little, whisp'ring, murm'ring shell, say cans't thou tell to me
Good news of any stately ship that sails upon the sea?
I press my ear, O little shell, against thy rosy lips;
Cans't tell me tales of those who go down to the sea in ships?

What, not a word? Ah hearken, shell, I've shut the cottage door;
There's scarce a sound to drown thy voice, so silent is the moor,
A bell may tinkle far away upon its purple rise;
A bee may buz among the heath—a lavrock cleave the skies.

But if you only breathe the name I name upon my knees,
Ah, surely I should catch the word above such sounds as these.
And Grannie's needles click no more, the ball of yarn is done,
And she's asleep outside the door where shines the merry sun.

One night while Grannie slept, I dreamed he came across the moor,
And stood, so handsome, brown and tall, beside the open door;

I thought I turned to pick a rose that by the sill had blown,
(He liked a rose) and when I looked, O shell, I was alone!

Across the moor there dwells a wife; she spaed my fortune true,
And said I'd plight my troth with one who wore a jacket blue;
That morn before my Grannie woke, just when the lapwing stirred,
I sped across the misty rise and sought the old wife's word.

With her it was the milking time, and while she milk'd the goat,
I ask'd her then to spae my dream, my heart was in my throat—
But that was just because the way had been so steep and long,
And not because I had the fear that anything was wrong.

"Ye'll meet, ye'll meet," was all she said; "Ye'll meet when it is mirk."
I gave her tippence that I meant for Sabbath-day and kirk;
And then I hastened back again; it seemed that never sure
The happy sun delay'd so long to gild the purple moor.

That's six months back, and every night I sit beside the door,
And while I knit I keep my gaze upon the mirky moor;

I keep old Collie by my side—he's sure to spring and bark,
When Ronald comes across the moor to meet me in the dark.

I *know* the old wife spaed me true, for did she not foretell
I'd break a ring with Ronald Grey beside the Hidden Well?
It came to pass at shearing-time, before he went to sea
(We're nighbours' bairns) how *could* she know that Ronald cared for me.

So night by night I watch for him—by day I sing and work,
And try to never mind the latch—he's coming in the dark;
Yet as the days and weeks and months go slipping slowly thro',
I wonder if the wise old wife has spaed my fortune true!

Ah, not a word about his ship? Well, well, I'll lay thee by.
I see a heron from the marsh go sailing in the sky,
The purple moor is like a dream, a star is twinkling clear—
Perhaps the meeting that she spaed is drawing very near!

TWO SONGS OF SPAIN.

Fountain, cans't thou sing the song
  My Juan sang to me
The moonlit orange groves among?
  Then list the words from me,
And mark thee, by the morning's light,
  Or by the moon's soft beam,
Or when my eyes with smiles are bright,
  Or when I wake or dream.
O, Fountain, thou must sing the song
  My Juan sang to me;
Yet stay—the only words I know
  Are "Inez, Love and Thee!"

Fountain, on my light guitar
  I'll play the strain to thee,
And while I watch yon laughing star,
  The words will come to me.
And mark thee, when my heart is sad,
  And full of sweet regrets,
Or when it throbs to laughter glad,
  Like feet to castanets.
O, Fountain, thou must sing the song
  My Juan sang to me;
Yet stay—the only words I know
  Are " Inez, Love, and Thee!"

TWO SONGS OF SPAIN.

Fountain, clap thy twinkling hands
   Beneath yon floating moon,
And twinkle to the starry bands
   That dance upon the gloom,
For I am glad, for who could crave,
   The joyous night to fill,
A richer treasure than I have
   In Juan's seguedille?
So, Fountain, mark, no other song
   Dare ever sing to me,
Tho' only four short words I know,
   Just, "Inez, Love and Thee!"

Morello strikes on his guitar,
When over the olives the star
Of eve, like a rose touch'd with gold,
Doth slowly its sweet rays unfold.
Perchance 'tis in some city square,
And the people all follow us there.
Don, donna, slim chulo, padrone,
The very dog runs with his bone;
One half of the square is in the shade,
On the other the red sunset fades;
The fount, as it flings up its jets,
Responds to my brisk castanets;
I wear a red rose at my ear;
And many a whisper I hear:
"If she were a lady, behold,
None other should share my red gold!"

"St. Anthony save us, what eyes!
How gem-like her little foot flies!"
"These dancers should all be forbid
To dance in the streets of Madrid."
"If I were a monarch I'd own
No other to sit on my throne!"
Two scarlet streamers tie my hair;
They burn like red stars on the air;
My dark eyes flash, my clear cheek burns,
My kirtle eddies in swift turns,
My golden necklet tinkles sweet;
Yes, yes, I love the crowded street!

THE CITY TREE.

I stand within the stony, arid town,
   I gaze for ever on the narrow street;
I hear for ever passing up and down,
   The ceaseless tramp of feet.

I know no brotherhood with far-lock'd woods,
   Where branches bourgeon from a kindred sap;
Where o'er moss'd roots, in cool, green solitudes,
   Small silver brooklets lap.

No em'rald vines creep wistfully to me,
   And lay their tender fingers on my bark;
High may I toss my boughs, yet never see
   Dawn's first most glorious spark.

THE CITY TREE.

When to and fro my branches wave and sway,
   Answ'ring the feeble wind that faintly calls,
They kiss no kindred boughs but touch alway
   The stones of climbing walls.

My heart is never pierc'd with song of bird;
   My leaves know nothing of that glad unrest,
Which makes a flutter in the still woods heard,
   When wild birds build a nest.

There never glance the eyes of violets up,
   Blue into the deep splendour of my green:
Nor falls the sunlight to the primrose cup,
   My quivering leaves between.

Not mine, not mine to turn from soft delight
   Of wood-bine breathings, honey sweet, and warm;
With kin embattl'd rear my glorious height
   To greet the coming storm!

Not mine to watch across the free, broad plains
   The whirl of stormy chorts sweeping fast;
The level, silver lances of great rains,
   Blown onward by the blast.

Not mine the clamouring tempest to defy,
   Tossing the proud crest of my dusky leaves:
Defender of small flowers that trembling lie
   Against my barky greaves.

Not mine to watch the wild swan drift above,
   Balanced on wings that could not choose between
The wooing sky, blue as the eye of love,
   And my own tender green.

And yet my branches spread, a kingly sight,
　In the close prison of the drooping air:
When sun-vex'd noons are at their fiery height,
　My shade is broad, and there

Come city toilers, who their hour of ease
　Weave out to precious seconds as they lie
Pillow'd on horny hands, to hear the breeze
　Through my great branches die.

I see no flowers, but as the children race
　With noise and clamour through the dusty street,
I see the bud of many an angel face—
　I hear their merry feet.

No violets look up, but shy and grave,
　The children pause and lift their chrystal eyes
To where my emerald branches call and wave—
　As to the mystic skies.

LATE LOVED—WELL LOVED.

He stood beside her in the dawn
　(And she his Dawn and she his Spring),
From her bright palm she fed her fawn,
　Her swift eyes chased the swallow's wing:
Her restless lips, smile-haunted, cast
　Shrill silver calls to hound and dove:
Her young locks wove them with the blast.
　To the flush'd, azure shrine above,

The light boughs o'er her golden head
  Toss'd em'rald arm and blossom palm,
The perfume of their prayer was spread
  On the sweet wind in breath of balm.

" Dawn of my heart," he said, " O child,
  Knit thy pure eyes a space with mine :
O chrystal, child eyes, undefiled,
  Let fair love leap from mine to thine !"
'The Dawn is young," she smiled and said,
  " Too young for Love's dear joy and woe ;
Too young to crown her careless head
  With his ripe roses. Let me go—
Unquestion'd for a longer space,
  Perchance, when day is at the flood,
In thy true palm I'll gladly place
  Love's flower in its rounding bud.
But now the day is all too young,
  The Dawn and I are playmates still."
She slipped the blossomed boughs among,
  He strode beyond the violet hill.

Again they stand (Imperial noon
  Lays her red sceptre on the earth),
Where golden hangings make a gloom,
  And far off lutes sing dreamy mirth.
The peacocks cry to lily cloud,
  From the white gloss of balustrade :
Tall urns of gold the gloom make proud,
  Tall statues whitely strike the shade,
And pulse in the dim quivering light
  Until, most Galatea-wise—

Each looks from base of malachite
    With mystic life in limbs and eyes.

Her robe (a golden wave that rose,
    And burst, and clung as water clings
To her long curves) about her flows.
    Each jewel on her white breast sings
Its silent song of sun and fire.
    No wheeling swallows smite the skies
And upward draw the faint desire,
    Weaving its myst'ry in her eyes.
In the white kisses of the tips
    Of her long fingers lies a rose,
Snow-pale beside her curving lips,
    Red by her snowy breast it glows.

"Noon of my soul," he says, "behold !
    The day is ripe, the rose full blown,
Love stands in panoply of gold,
    To Jovian height and strength now grown.
No infant he, a king he stands,
    And pleads with thee for love again."
"Ah, yes !" she says, "in known lands,
    He kings it—lord of subtlest pain ;
The moon is full, the rose is fair—
    Too fair ! 'tis neither white nor red :
"I know the rose that love should wear,
    Must redden as the heart had bled !
The moon is mellow bright, and I
    Am happy in its perfect glow.
The slanting sun the rose may dye—
    But for the sweet noon—let me go."

She parted—shimm'ring thro' the shade,
   Bent the fair splendour of her head :
"Would the rich noon were past," he said,
   Would the pale rose were flush'd to red!"

Again. The noon is past and night
   Binds on his brow the blood red Mars—
Down dusky vineyards dies the fight,
   And blazing hamlets slay the stars.
Shriek the shrill shells : the heated throats
   Of thunderous canon burst—and high
Scales the fierce joy of bugle notes :
   The flame-dimm'd splendours of the sky.
He, dying, lies beside his blade :
   Clear smiling as a warrior blest
With victory smiles, thro' sinister shade
   Gleams the White Cross upon her breast.

"Soul of my soul, or is it night
   Or is it dawn or is it day ?
I see no more nor dark nor light,
   I hear no more the distant fray."
"'Tis Dawn," she whispers : " Dawn at last !
   Bright flush'd with love's immortal glow
For me as thee, all earth is past !
   Late loved—well loved, now let us go !"

LA BOUQUETIÉRE.

Buy my roses, citizens,—
    Here are roses golden white,
Like the stars that lovers watch
    On a purple summer night.
Here are roses ruddy red,
    Here are roses Cupid's pink ;
Here are roses like his cheeks—
    Deeper—like his lips, I think.
Vogue la galère ! what if they die,
Roses will bloom again—so, buy !

Here is one—it should be white ;
    As tho' in a playful mind,
Flora stole the winter snow
    From the sleeping north'rn wind ;
And lest he should wake and rage,
    Breath'd a spell of ardent pow'r
On the flake, and flung it down
    To the earth, a snow-white flow'r.
Vogue la galère ! 'tis stain'd with red ?
That only means—a woman's dead !

Buy my flowers, citizens,—
    Here's a Parma violet ;
Ah ! why is my white rose red ?
    'Tis the blood of a grisette ;
She sold her flowers by the quay ;
    Brown her eyes and fair her hair ;

LA BOQUETIERE.

Sixteen summers old, I think—
   With a quaint, Provincial air.
Vogue la galère ! she's gone the way
That flesh as well as flow'rs must stray.

She had a father old and lame ;
   He wove his baskets by her side ;
Well, well ! 'twas fair enough to see
   Her look of love, his glance of pride ;
He wore a beard of shaggy grey,
   And clumsy patches on his blouse ;
She wore about her neck a cross,
   And on her feet great wooden shoes.
Vogue la galère ! we have no cross,
Th' Republic says it's gold is dross !

They had a dog, old, lame, and lean ;
   He once had been a noble hound ;
And day by day he lay and starv'd,
   Or gnaw'd some bone that he had found.
They shar'd with him the scanty crust,
   That barely foil'd starvation's pain ;
He'd wag his feeble tail and turn
   To gnaw that polish'd bone again.
Vogue la galère ! why don't ye greet
My tale with laughter, prompt and meet?

No fear ! ye'll chorus me with laughs
   When draws my long jest to its close—
And have for life a merry joke,
   " The spot of blood upon the rose."

LA BOQUETIERE.

She sold her flow'rs—but what of that?
   The child was either good or dense;
She starv'd—for one she would not sell,
   Patriots, 'twas her innocence!
Vogue la galère! poor little clod!
Like us, she could not laugh at God.

A week ago I saw a crowd
   Of red-caps; and a Tricoteuse
Call'd as I hurried swiftly past—
   "They've taken little Wooden Shoes!"
Well, so they had. Come, laugh, I say;
   Your laugh with mine should come in pat!
For she, the little sad-fac'd child,
   Was an accurs'd aristocrat!
Vogue la galère! the Republic's said
Saints, angels, nobles, all are dead.

"The old man, too!" shriek'd out the crowd;
   She turn'd her small white face about;
And ye'd have laugh'd to see the air
   With which she fac'd that rabble rout!
I laugh'd, I know—some laughter breeds
   A merry moisture in the eye:
My cheeks were wet, to see her hand
   Try to push those brawny patriots by.
Vogue la galère! we'll laugh nor weep
When Death, not God, calls *us* to sleep.

"Not Jean!" she said, "'tis only I
   That noble am—take only me;

I only am his foster-child,—
   He nurs'd me on his knee!
See! he is guiltless of the crime
   Of noble birth—and lov'd me not,
Because I claim an old descent,
   But that he nurs'd me in his cot!"
Vogue la galère! 'tis well no God
Exists, to look upon this sod!

"Believe her not!" he shriek'd; "O, no!
   I am the father of her life!"
"Poor Jean!" she said; "believe him not,
   His mind with dreams is rife.
Farewell, dear Jean!" she said. I laugh'd,
   Her air was so sedately grand.
"Thou'st been a faithful servant, so
   Thou well may'st kiss my hand."
Vogue la galère! the sun is red—
And will be, Patriots, when we're dead.

"Child! my dear child!" he shriek'd; she turn'd
   And let the patriots close her round;
He was so lame, he fell behind—
   He and the starving hound.
"Let him go free!" yell'd out the mob;
   "Accurs'd be these nobles all!
The poor old wretch is craz'd it seems;
   Blood, Citizens, *will* pall.
Vogue la galère! We can't buy wine,
So let blood flow—be't thine or mine."

I ply my trade about the Place
   Where proudly reigns La Guillotine;

I pile my basket up with bloom,
  With mosses soft and green.
This morning, not an hour ago,
  I stood beside a Tricoteuse;
And saw the little fair head fall
  Off the little Wooden Shoes.
Vogue la galère! By Sanson's told,
Into his basket, dross and gold.

She died alone. A woman drew
  As close beside her as she might;
And in that woman's basket lay
  A rose all snowy white.
But sixteen summers old—a child
  As one might say—to die alone;
Ah, well—it is the only way
  These nobles can atone!
Vogue la galère! here is my jest—
My white rose redden'd from her breast!

Buy my roses, Citizens!
  Here's a vi'let—here's a pink—
Deeper tint than Cupid's cheek;
  Deeper than his lips, I think.
Flora's nymphs on rosy feet
  Ne'er o'er brighter blossoms sprang!
Ne'er a songster sweeter blooms,
  In his sweetest rhyming sang!
Vogue la galère! Roses must die—
Roses will grow again—so, buy!

CURTIUS.

How spake the Oracle, my Curtius, how?
Methought, while on the shadow'd terraces
I walked and looked towards Rome, an echo came,
Of legion wails, blent into one deep cry.
" O, Jove!" I thought, " the Oracles have said ;
And saying, touched some swiftly answering chord,
Gen'ral to ev'ry soul." And then my heart
(I being here alone) beat strangely loud ;
Responsive to the cry—and my still soul,
Inform'd me thus : " Not such a harmony
Could spring from aught within the souls of men,"
But that which is most common to all souls.
Lo! that is sorrow!" "Nay, Curtius, I could smile,
To tell thee as I listen'd to the cry,
How on the silver flax which blew about
The ivory distaff in my languid hand,
I found large tears ; such big and rounded drops
As gather thro' dark nights on cypress boughs,
And I was sudden anger'd, for I thought :
" Why should a gen'ral wail come home to me
With such vibration in my trembling heart,
That such great tears should rise and overflow?"
Then shook them on the marble where I pac'd ;
Where instantly they vanished in the sun,
As di'monds fade in flames, 'twas foolish, Curtius!
And then methought how strange and lone it seem'd,
For till thou cam'st I seem'd to be alone,

On the vin'd terrace, prison'd in the gold
Of that still noontide hour. No widows stole
Up the snow-glimmering marble of the steps
To take my alms and bless the Gods and me;
No orphans touched the fringes of my robe
With innocent babe-fingers, nor dropped the gold
I laid in their soft palms, to laugh, and stroke
The jewels on my neck, or touch the rose
Thou sayest, Curtius, lives upon my cheek.
Perchance all lingered in the Roman streets
To catch first tidings from the Oracles.
The very peacocks drows'd in distant shades,
Nor sought my hand for honey'd cake; and high
A hawk sailed blackly in the clear blue sky,
And kept my doves from cooing at my feet.
My lute lay there, bound with the small white buds,
Which, laughing this bright morn, thou brought and wreath'd
Around it as I sang—but with that wail
Dying across the vines and purple slopes,
And breaking on its strings, I did not care
To waken music, nor in truth could force
My voice or fingers to it, so I stray'd
Where hangs thy best loved armour on the wall,
And pleased myself by filling it with thee!
'Tis yet the goodliest armour in proud Rome,
Say all the armourers; all Rome and I
Know *thee*, the lordliest bearer of a sword.
Yet, Curtius, stay, there is a rivet lost
From out the helmet, and a ruby gone
From the short sword hilt—trifles both which can
Be righted by to-morrow's noon—" to-morrow's noon !"

Was there a change, my Curtius, in my voice
When spake I those three words: "to-morrow's noon?"
O, I am full of dreams—methought there was.
"Why, love, how darkly gaze thine eyes in mine!
If lov'd I dismal thoughts I well could deem
Thou saw'st not the blue of my fond eyes,
But look'd between the lips of that dread pit—
O, Jove! to name it seems to curse the air
With chills of death—we'll not speak of it, Curtius.
When I had dimm'd thy shield with kissing it,
I went between the olives to the stalls;
White Audax neigh'd out to me as I came,
As I had been Hippona to his eyes;
New dazzling from the one, small, mystic cloud
That like a silver chariot floated low
In the ripe blue of noon, and seem'd to pause,
Stay'd by the hilly round of yon aged tree.
He stretch'd the ivory arch of his vast neck,
Smiting sharp thunders from the marble floor
With hoofs impatient of a peaceful earth;
Shook the long silver of his burnish'd mane,
Until the sunbeams smote it into light,
Such as a comet trails across the sky.
I love him, Curtius! Such magnanimous fires
Leap from his eyes. I do truly think
That with thee seated on him, thy strong knees
Against his sides—the bridle in his jaws
In thy lov'd hand, to pleasure thee he'd spring
Sheer from the verge of Earth into the breast
Of Death and Chaos—of Death and Chaos!—
What omens seem to strike my soul to-day?

What is there in this blossom-hour should knit
An omen in with ev'ry simple word?
Should make yon willows with their hanging locks
Dusk sybils, mutt'ring sorrows to the air?
The roses clamb'ring round yon marble Pan,
Wave like red banners floating o'er the dead?
The dead—there 'tis again. My Curtius, come
And thou shalt tell me of the Oracles
And what sent hither that long cry of woe.
Yet wait, yet wait, I care not much to hear.
While on thy charger's throbbing neck I lean'd,
Romeward there pass'd across the violet slopes,
Five sacrificial bulls, with silver hides,
And horns as cusp'd and white as Dian's bow,
And lordly breasts which laid the honey'd thyme
Into long swarths, whence smoke of yellow bees
Rose up in puffs, dispersing as it rose,
For the great temple they; and as they pass'd
With quiet gait, I heard their drivers say:
The bulls were for the Altars, when should come
Word from the Oracles, as to the Pit,
O, Curtius, Curtius, in my soul I see
How black and fearful is its glutton throat;
I will not look!
O, Soul, be blind and see not! Then the men
Wav'd their long goads, still juicy from the vine,
And plum'd with bronzy leaves, and each to each,
Showed the sleek beauty of the rounded sides,
The mighty curving of the lordly breasts,
The level lines of backs, the small, fine heads.
And laugh'd and said, " The Gods will have it thus,

The choicest of the earth for sacrifice;
Let it be man, or maid, or lowing bull!"
Where lay the witchcraft in their clownish words,
To shake my heart? I know not; but it thrill'd,
As Daphne's leaves, thrill to a wind so soft,
One might not feel it on the open palm;
I cannot choose but laugh—for what have I
To do with altars and with sacrifice?

THE FARMER'S DAUGHTER CHERRY.

The Farmer quit what he was at,
    The bee-hive he was smokin':
He tilted back his old straw hat—
    Says he, "Young man, you're jokin'!
O Lordy! (Lord, forgive the swar,)
    Ain't ye a cheeky sinner?
Come, if I give my gal thar,
    Where would *you* find her dinner?

"Now look at *me*; I settl'd down
    When I was one and twenty,
Me, and my axe and Mrs. Brown,
    And stony land a plenty.
Look up thar! ain't that homestead fine,
    And look at them thar cattle:
I tell ye since that early time
    I've fit a tidy battle.

"It kinder wrestles down a man
  To fight the stuns and mire:
But I sort of clutch'd to thet thar plan
  Of David and Goliar.
Want was the mean old Philistine
  That strutted round the clearin',
Of pebbles I'd a hansum line,
  And flung 'em nothin' fearin'.

"They hit him square, right whar they ought,
  Them times I *had* an arm!
I lick'd the giant and I bought
  A hundred acre farm.
My gal was born about them days,
  I was mowin' in the medder;
When some one comes along and says—
  "The wife's gone thro' the shadder!"

"Times thought it was God's will she went—
  Times thought she work'd too slavin'—
And for the young one that was sent,
  I took to steady savin'.
Jest cast your eye on that thar hill
  The sugar bush just tetches,
And round by Miller Jackson's mill,
  All round the farm stretches.

"'Ain't got a mind to give that land
  To any snip-snap feller
That don't know loam from mud or sand,
  Or if corn's blue or yaller.

I've got a mind to keep her yet—
  Last Fall her cheese and butter
Took prizes; sakes! I can't forget
  Her pretty pride and flutter.

" Why, you be off! her little face
  For me's the only summer;
Her gone, 'twould be a queer, old place,
  The Lord smile down upon her!
All goes with her, the house and lot—
  You'd like to get 'em, very!
I'll give 'em when this maple bears
  A bouncin' ripe-red cherry!"

The Farmer fixed his hat and specks
  And pursed his lips together,
The maple wav'd above his head,
  Each gold and scarlet feather:
The Teacher's honest heart sank down:
  How could his soul be merry?
He knew—though teaching in a town,
  No maple bears a cherry.

Soft blew the wind; the great old tree,
  Like Saul to David's singing,
Nodded its jewelled crown, as he
  Swayed to the harp-strings' ringing;
A something rosy—not a leaf
  Stirs up amid the branches;
A miracle *may* send relief
  To lovers fond and anxious!

O rosy is the velvet cheek
  Of one 'mid red leaves sitting !
The sunbeams played at hide-and-seek
  With the needles in her knitting.
" O Pa !" The Farmer prick'd his ears,
  Whence came that voice so merry ?
(The Teacher's thoughtful visage clears)
  " The maple bears a cherry !"

The Farmer tilted back his hat :
  " Well, gal—as I'm a human,
I'll always hold as doctrine that
  Thar's nothin' beats a woman !
When crown'd that maple is with snow,
  And Christmas bells are merry,
I'll let you have her, Jack—that's so !
  Be sure you're good to Cherry !

SOME OF FARMER STEBBIN'S OPINIONS.

No, Parson, 'tain't been in my style,
  (Nor none ov my relations)
Tew dig about the gnarly roots
  Ov prophetic spekkleations,
Tew see what Malachai meant ;
  Or Solomon was hintin' ;
Or reound what jog o' Futur's road
  Isaiah was a-squintin'.

I've lost my rest a-keepin' out
   The hogs from our cowcumbers ;
But never lost a wink, you bet,
   By wrastlin' over Numbers.
I never took no comfort when
   The year was bald with losses,
A-spekkleatin' on them chaps
   That rode them varus hosses.

It never gave my soul a boost
   When grief an' it was matin',
Tew figger out that that thar Pope
   Wus reely twins with Satan.
I took no stock in countin' up
   How menny hed ov cattle
From Egypt's ranches Moses drove ;
   I never fit a battle
On p'ints that frequently gave rise
   Tew pious spat an' grumble,
An' makes the brethren clinch an' yell
   In spiritooal rough-an'-tumble.

I never bet on Paul agin
   The argyments ov Peter,
I never made the good old Book
   A kind ov moral teeter ;
Tew pass a choreless hour away,
   An' get the evenin' over ;
I swallered it jest as it stood,
   From cover clar tew cover.

Hain't had no time tew disputate,
  Except with axe an' arm,
With stump an' rampike and with stuns,
  Upon my half clar'd farm.
An' when sech argyments as them—
  Fill six days out ov seven;
A man on Sabbath wants tew crawl
  By quiet ways tew heaven.

Again he gets the waggon out,
  An' hitches up the sorrels,
An' rides ten miles tew meetin', he
  Ain't braced for pious quarrels:
No, sir, he ain't! that waggon rolls
  From corduroy to puddle,
An' that thar farmer gets his brains
  Inter an easy muddle.

His back is stiff from six days' toil—
  So God takes hold an' preaches,
In boughs ov rustlin' maple an'
  In whisperin' leaves ov beeches:
Sez He tew that thar farmin' chap
  (Likewise tew the old woman),
"I guess I'm built tew comprehend
  That you an' her be's human!"

"So jest take hold on this har day,
  Recowperate yer muscle;
Let up a mite this day on toil,
  'Taint made for holy bustle.

Let them old sorrels jog along,
  With mighty slack-like traces ;
Half dreamin', es my sunbeams fleck
  Their venerable faces.

" I guess they did their share ov work,
  Since Monday's dew was hoary ;
Don't try tew lick 'em tew a trot
  Upon the road tew Glory !
Jest let 'em laze a spell whar thick
  My lily-buds air blowin' :
An' whar My trees cast shadders on
  My silver creeklet flowin'.

" An' while their red, rough tongues push back
  The stems ov reed an' lily,
Jest let 'em dream ov them thar days
  When they was colt an' filly,
An' spekkleate, es fetlock deep
  They eye my cool creek flowin',
On whar I loosed it from My hand,
  Where be its crisp waves goin'.
An' how in snow-white lily cup
  I built them yaller fires,
An' bronz'd them reeds that rustle up
  Agin the waggon tires.

" An' throw a forrard eye along
  Where that bush roadway passes,
A-spekkleating on the chance—
  Ov nibbling road-side grasses.

Jest let them lines rest on thar necks—
  Restrain yer moral twitters—
An' paste this note inside yer hat—
  I talk tew all My critters !

" Be they on four legs or on two,
  In broadcloth, scales or feathers,
No matter what may be the length
  Ov all their mental tethers :
In ways mayn't suit the minds ov them
  That thinks themselves thar betters.
I talk tew them in simple style,
  In words ov just three letters,—
Spell'd out in lily-blow an' reed,
  In soft winds on them blowin',
In juicy grass by wayside streams,
  In coolin' waters flowin'.

" An' so jest let them sorrels laze
  My ripplin' silver creek in ;
They're listenin' in thar own dumb way,
  An' I—Myself—am speakin' ;
Friend Stebbens, don't you feel your soul
  In no sort ov dejection ;
You'll get tew meetin' quick enough,
  In time for the—collection."

THE DEACON AND HIS DAUGHTER.

He saved his soul and saved his pork,
  With old time preservation ;
He did not hold with creosote,
  Or new plans of salvation ;
He said that " Works would show the man,"
" The smoke-house tell upon the ham !"

He didn't, when he sunk a well,
  Inspect the stuns and gravel ;
To prove that Moses was a dunce,
  Unfit for furrin travel ;
He marvell'd at them works of God—
An' broke 'em up to mend the road !

And when the Circus come around,
  He hitch'd his sleek old horses ;
And in his rattlin' wagon took
  His dimpl'd household forces—
The boys to wonder at the Clown,
And think his fate Life's highest crown.

He wondered at the zebras wild,
  Nor knew 'em painted donkeys ;
An' when he gave the boys a dime
  For cakes to feed the monkeys,
He never thought, in any shape,
He had descended from an ape !

THE DEACON AND HIS DAUGHTER.

And when he saw some shallow-pate,
  With smallest brain possession,
He uttered no filosofy
  On Nature's retrogression.
To ancient types, by Darwin's rule,
He simply said, " Wal, darn a fool !"

He never had an enemy,
  But once a year to meetin',
When he and Deacon Maybee fought
  On questions of free seatin';
Or which should be the one t' rebuke
Pastor for kissin' sister Luke.

His farm was well enough, but stones
  Kind of stern, ruthless facts is ;
An' he jest made out to save a mite,
  An' pay his righteous taxes,
An' mebbe tote some flour an' pork
To poor old critters past their work.

But on the neatest thing he hed
  Around the place or dwellin',
I guess he never paid a red
  Of taxes. No mush melon
Was rounder, sweeter, pinker than
The old man's daughter, Minta Ann.

I've been at Philadelfy's show
  An' other similar fusses,
An' seen a mighty sight of stone,
  Minarveys and Venusses ;

An' Sikeys clad in flowers an' wings,
But not much show of factory things.

I've seen the hull entire crowd
　　Of Jove's female relations,
An' I feel to make a solemn swear
　　On them thar " Lamentations,"
That as a sort of general plan
I'd rather spark with Minta Ann !

You'd ought to see her dimpled chin,
　　With one red freckle on it,
Her brown eyes glancing underneath
　　Her tilted shaker bonnet.
I vow, I often did desire,
They'd set the plaguey thing a-fire !

You'd ought to hear that gal sing
　　On Sabbath, up to meetin',
You'd kind of feel high lifted up,
　　Your soul for Heaven fleetin'.
And then—came supper, down she'd tie
You to this earth with pumpkin pie !

I tell you, stranger, 'twas a sight
　　For poetry and speeches,
To see her sittin' on the stoop,
　　A-peelin' scarlet peaches,
Inter the kettle at her feet,—
I tell you, 'twas a show complete !

Drip, droppin' thro' the rustlin' vine,
　　The sunbeams came a flittin' ;

An' sort of danced upon the floor,
    Chas'd by the tabby kitten;
Losh! to see the critter's big surprise,
When them beams slipped into Minta's eyes!

An' down her brow her pretty hair
    Cum curlin', crinklin', creepin',
In leetle, yaller mites of rings,
    Inter them bright eyes peepin',
Es run the tendrils of the vine,
To whar the merry sunbeams shine.

But losh! her smile was dreadful shy,
    An' kept her white lids under;
Jest as when darkens up the sky
    An' growls away the thunder;
Them skeery speckled trout will hide
Beneath them white pond lilies' pride!

An' then her heart, 'twas made clar through
    Of Californy metal,
Chock full of things es sugar sweet
    Es a presarvin' kettle.
The beaux went crazed fur menny a mile
When I got thet kettle on the bile.

The good old deacon's gone to whar
    Thar ain't no wild contentions
On Buildin' Funds' Committees and
    No taxes nor exemptions.
Yet still I sort of feel he preaches,
And Minta Ann preserves my peaches.

SAID THE SKYLARK.

"O soft, small cloud, the dim, sweet dawn adorning,
Swan-like a-sailing on its tender grey;
    Why dost thou, dost thou float,
    So high, the wing'd, wild note
Of silver lamentation from my dark and pulsing throat
    May never reach thee,
    Tho' every note beseech thee
To bend thy white wings downward thro' the smiling of
                                  [the morning,
And by the black wires of my prison lightly stray?

"O dear, small cloud, when all blue morn is ringing
With sweet notes piped from other throats than mine;
    If those glad singers please
    The tall and nodding trees—
If to them dance the pennants of the swaying columbine,
    If to their songs are set
The dance of daffodil and trembling violet—
    Will they pursue thee
With tireless wings as free and bold as thine?
    Will they woo thee
With love throbs in the music of their singing?
    Ah, nay! fair Cloud, ah, nay!
    Their hearts and wings will stay
With yellow bud of primrose and soft blush of the May;
    Their songs will thrill and die,

Tranc'd in the perfume of the rose's breast,
    While I must see thee fly
With white, broad, lonely pinions down the sky.

" O fair, small cloud, unheeding o'er me straying,
Jewell'd with topaz light of fading stars ;
    Thy downy edges red
As the great eagle of the Dawn sails high
    And sets his fire-bright head
And wind-blown pinions towards thy snowy breast ;
    And thou canst blush while I
    Must pierce myself with song and die
On the bald sod behind my prison bars ;
    Nor feel upon my crest
Thy soft, sunn'd touches delicately playing !

" O fair, small cloud, grown small as lily flow'r !
Even while I smite the bars to see thee fade ;
    The wind shall bring thee
    The strain I sing thee—
I, in wired prison stay'd,
Worse than the breathless primrose glade.
    That in my morn,
    I shrilly sang to scorn ;
I'll burst my heart up to thee in this hour !

" O fair, small cloud, float nearer yet and hear me !
A prison'd lark once lov'd a snowy cloud,
    Nor did the Day
    With sapphire lips, and kiss
    Of summery bliss,

Draw all her soul away ;
    Vainly the fervent East
Deck'd her with roses for their bridal feast ;
    She would not rest
In his red arms, but slipp'd adown the air
    And wan and fair,
Her light foot touch'd a purple mountain crest,
    And touching, turn'd
Into swift rain, that like to jewels burn'd ;
In the great, wondering azure of the sky ;
    And while a rainbow spread
Its mighty arms above, she, singing, fled
    To the lone-feather'd slave,
    In his sad weird grave,
Whose heart upon his silver song had sped
    To her in days of old,
    In dawns of gold,
And murmuring to him, said :
" O love, I come ! O love, I come to cheer thee—
    Love, to be near thee !"

WAR.

Shake, shake the earth with giant tread,
    Thou red-maned Titian bold ;
For every step a man lies dead,
    A cottage hearth is cold.

WAR.

Take up the babes with mailed hands,
  Transfix them with thy spears,
Spare not the chaste young virgin-bands,
  Tho' blood may be their tears.

Beat down the corn, tear up the vine,
  The waters turn to blood;
And if the wretch for bread doth whine,
  Give him his kin for food.
Aye, strew the dead to saddle girth,
  They make so rich a mould,
Thoul't thus enrich the wasted earth—
  They'll turn to yellow gold.

On with thy thunders, shot and shell,
  Send screaming, featly hurl'd;
Science has made them in her cell,
  To *civilize* the world.
Not, not alone where Christian men
  Pant in the well-arm'd strife;
But seek the jungle-throttled glen—
  The savage has a life.

He has a soul—so priests will say—
  Go! save it with thy sword;
Thro' his rank forests force thy way,
  Thy war cry, "For the Lord!"
Rip up his mines, and from his strands
  Wash out the gold with blood—
Religion raises blessing hands,
  "War's evil worketh good!"

When striding o'er the conquer'd land,
  Silence thy rolling drum,
And led by white-robed choiring bands
  With loud " *Te Deum* " come.
Seek the grim chancel, on its wall
  Thy blood-stiff banner hang;
They lie who say thy blood is gall,
  Thy tooth the serpent's fang.

See! the white Christ is lifted high,
  Thy conqu'ring sword to bless ;
Smiles the pure monarch of the sky—
  Thy king can do no less.
Drink deep with him the festal wine,
  Drink with him drop for drop ;
If, like the sun, his throne doth shine,
  Thou art that throne's prop.

If spectres wait upon the bowl,
  Thou needs not be afraid,
Grin hell-hounds for thy bold black soul,
  His purple be thy shade.
Go! feast with Commerce, be her spouse ;
  She loves thee, thou art hers—
For thee she decks her board and house,
  Then how may others curse

If she, mild-seeming matron, leans
  Upon thine iron neck,
And leaves with thee her household scenes
  To follow at thy beck—

Bastard in brotherhood of kings,
  Their blood runs in thy veins,
For them the crowns, the sword that swings,
  For thee to hew their chains.

For thee the rending of the prey—
  They, jackals to the lion,
Tread after in the gory way
  Trod by the mightier scion.
O slave! that slayest other slaves,
  O'er vassals crowned, a king!
War, build high thy throne with graves,
  High as the vulture's wing!

THE SWORD.

THE FORGING OF THE SWORD.

At the forging of the Sword—
  The mountain roots were stirr'd,
  Like the heart-beats of a bird;
  Like flax the tall trees wav'd,
So fiercely struck the Forgers of the Sword.

At the forging of the Sword—
  So loud the hammers fell,
  The thrice seal'd gates of Hell,
  Burst wide their glowing jaws;
Deep roaring, at the forging of the Sword.

THE SWORD.

At the forging of the Sword—
    Kind mother Earth was rent,
    Like an Arab's dusky tent,
    And monster-like she fed
On her children; at the forging of the Sword.

At the forging of the Sword—
    So loud the blows they gave,
    Up sprang the panting wave;
    And blind and furious slew,
Shrill-shouting to tne Forgers of the Sword.

At the forging of the Sword—
    The startled air swift whirl'd
    The red flames round the world,
    From the Anvil where was smitten,
The steel, the Forgers wrought into the Sword.

At the forging of the Sword—
    The Maid and Matron fled,
    And hid them with the dead;
    Fierce prophets sang their doom,
More deadly, than the wounding of the Sword.

At the forging of the Sword—
    Swift leap'd the quiet hearts,
    In the meadows and the marts;
    The tides of men were drawn,
By the gleaming sickle-planet of the Sword!

Thus wert thou forged, O lissome sword;
    On such dusk anvil wert thou wrought;

In such red flames thy metal fused !
  From such deep hells that metal brought ;
O sword, dread lord, thou speak'st no word,
But dumbly rul'st, king and lord !

Less than the Gods by some small span,
  Slim sword, how great thy lieges be !
Glint but in *one* wild camp-fire's light,
  Thy God-like vassals rush to thee.
O sword, dread lord, thou speak'st no word,
But dumbly rul'st, king and lord !

Sharp, God, how vast thy altars be !
  Green vallies, sacrificial cups,
Flow with the purple lees of blood ;
  Its smoke is round the mountain tops.
O sword, dread lord, thou speak'st no word,
But dumbly rul'st, king and lord !

O amorous God, fierce lover thou !
  Bright sultan of a million brides,
Thou know'st no rival to *thy* kiss,
  Thy loves are *thine* whate're betides,
O sword, dread lord, thou speak'st no word,
But dumbly rul'st, king and lord.

Unflesh thee, sword ! No more, no more,
  Thy steel no more shall sting and shine,
Pass thro' the fusing fires again ;
  And learn to prune the laughing vine.
Fall sword, dread lord, with one accord,
The plough and hook we'll own as lord !

ROSES IN MADRID.

Roses, Senors, roses!
　Love is subtly hid
In the fragrant roses,
　Blown in gay Madrid.
Roses, Senors, roses!
　Look, look, look, and see
Love hanging in the roses,
　Like a golden bee!
Ha! ha! shake the roses—
　Hold a palm below;
Shake him from the roses,
　Catch the vagrant so!

High I toss the roses
　From my brown palm up;
Like the wine that bubbles
　From a golden cup.
Catch the roses, Senors,
　Light on finger tips;
He who buys red roses,
　Dreams of crimson lips!
Tinkle! my fresh roses,
　With the rare dews wet;
Clink! my crisp, red roses,
　Like a castanet!

Roses, Senors, roses,
  Come, Hidalgo, buy !
Proudly wait my roses
  For thy rose's eye.
Be thy rose as stately
  As a pacing deer ;
Worthy are my roses
  To burn behind her ear.
Ha ! ha ! I can see thee,
  Where the fountains foam,
Twining my red roses
  In her golden comb !

Roses, Donnas, roses,
  None so fresh as mine,
Pluck'd at rose of morning
  By our Lady's shrine.
Those that first I gather'd
  Laid I at her feet,
That is why my roses
  Still are fresh and sweet.
Roses, Donnas, roses !
  Roses waxen fair !
Acolytes my roses,
  Censing ladies' pray'r !

Roses, roses, roses !
  Hear the tawny bull
Thund'ring in the circus—
  Buy your arms full.

Roses by the dozen !
Roses by the score !
Pelt the victor with them—
Bull or Toreador !

BETWEEN THE WIND AND RAIN.

" The storm is in the air," she said, and held
Her soft palm to the breeze ; and looking up,
Swift sunbeams brush'd the crystal of her eyes,
As swallows leave the skies to skim the brown,
Bright woodland lakes. " The rain is in the air.
" O Prophet Wind, what hast thou told the rose,
" That suddenly she loosens her red heart,
" And sends long, perfum'd sighs about the place ?
" O Prophet Wind, what hast thou told the Swift,
" That from the airy eave, she, shadow-grey,
" Smites the blue pond, and speeds her glancing wing
" Close to the daffodils? What hast thou told small bells,
" And tender buds, that—all unlike the rose—
" They draw green leaves close, close about their breasts
" And shrink to sudden slumber ? The sycamores
" In ev'ry leaf are eloquent with thee ;
" The poplars busy all their silver tongues
" With answ'ring thee, and the round chestnut stirs
" Vastly but softly, at thy prophecies.
" The vines grow dusky with a deeper green—

"And with their tendrils snatch thy passing harp,
"And keep it by brief seconds in their leaves.
"O Prophet Wind, thou tellest of the rain,
"While, jacinth blue, the broad sky folds calm palms,
"Unwitting of all storm, high o'er the land !
"The little grasses and the ruddy heath
"Know of the coming rain ; but towards the sun
"The eagle lifts his eyes, and with his wings
"Beats on a sunlight that is never marr'd
"By cloud or mist, shrieks his fierce joy to air
"Ne'er stirr'd by stormy pulse."
"The eagle mine," I said : "O I would ride
"His wings like Ganymede, nor ever care
"To drop upon the stormy earth again,—
"But circle star-ward, narrowing my gyres,
"To some great planet of eternal peace."
"Nay," said my wise, young love, "the eagle falls
"Back to his cliff, swift as a thunder-bolt ;
"For there his mate and naked eaglets dwell,
"And there he rends the dove, and joys in all
"The fierce delights of his tempestuous home.
"And tho' the stormy Earth throbs thro' her poles—
"With tempests rocks upon her circling path—
"And bleak, black clouds snatch at her purple hills—
"While mate and eaglets shriek upon the rock—
"The eagle leaves the hylas to its calm,
"Beats the wild storm apart that rings the earth,
"And seeks his eyrie on the wind-dash'd cliff.
"O Prophet Wind ! close, close the storm and rain !"

Long sway'd the grasses like a rolling wave
Above an undertow—the mastiff cried ;

Low swept the poplars, groaning in their hearts;
And iron-footed stood the gnarl'd oaks,
And brac'd their woody thews against the storm.
Lash'd from the pond, the iv'ry cygnets sought
The carven steps that plung'd into the pool;
The peacocks scream'd and dragg'd forgotten plumes.
On the sheer turf—all shadows subtly died,
In one large shadow sweeping o'er the land;
Bright windows in the ivy blush'd no more;
The ripe, red walls grew pale—the tall vane dim;
Like a swift off'ring to an angry God,
O'erweighted vines shook plum and apricot,
From trembling trellis, and the rose trees pour'd
A red libation of sweet, ripen'd leaves,
On the trim walks. To the high dove-cote set
A stream of silver wings and violet breasts,
The hawk-like storm swooping on their track.
" Go," said my love, " the storm would whirl me off
" As thistle-down. I'll shelter here—but you—
" You love no storms!" " Where thou art," I said,
" Is all the calm I know—wert thou enthron'd
" On the pivot of the winds—or in the maelstrom,
" Thou holdest in thy hand my palm of peace;
" And, like the eagle, I would break the belts
" Of shouting tempests to return to thee,
" Were I above the storm on broad wings.
" Yet no she-eagle thou ! a small, white, lily girl
" I clasp and lift and carry from the rain,
" Across the windy lawn."
       With this I wove
Her floating lace about her floating hair,

And crush'd her snowy raiment to my breast,
And while she thought of frowns, but smil'd instead,
And wrote her heart in crimson on her cheeks,
I bounded with her up the breezy slopes,
The storm about us with such airy din,
As of a thousand bugles, that my heart
Took courage in the clamor, and I laid
My lips upon the flow'r of her pink ear,
And said : " I love thee ; give me love again !"
And here she pal'd, love has its dread, and then
She clasp'd its joy and redden'd in its light,
Till all the daffodils I trod were pale
Beside the small flow'r red upon my breast.
And ere the dial on the slope was pass'd,
Between the last loud bugle of the Wind
And the first silver coinage of the Rain,
Upon my flying hair, there came her kiss,
Gentle and pure upon my face—and thus
Were we betroth'd between the Wind and Rain.

JOY'S CITY.

Joy's City hath high battlements of gold ;
   Joy's City hath her streets of gem-wrought flow'rs ;
She hath her palaces high reared and bold,
   And tender shades of perfumed lily bowers ;
But ever day by day, and ever night by night,
An Angel measures still our City of Delight.

JOY'S CITY.

He hath a rule of gold, and never stays,
    But ceaseless round the burnish'd ramparts glides ;
He measures minutes of her joyous days,
    Her walls, her trees, the music of her tides ;
The roundness of her buds—Joy's own fair city lies,
Known to its heart-core by his stern and thoughtful eyes.

Above the sounds of timbrel and of song,
    Of greeting friends, of lovers 'mid the flowers,
The Angel's voice arises clear and strong :
    " O City, by so many leagues thy bow'rs
Stretch o'er the plains, and in the fair high-lifted blue
So many cubits rise thy tow'rs beyond the view."

Why dost thou, Angel, measure Joy's fair walls ?
    Unceasing gliding by their burnish'd stones ;
Go, rather measure Sorrow's gloomy halls ;
    Her cypress bow'rs, her charnel-house of bones ;
Her groans, her tears, the rue in her jet chalices ;
But leave unmeasured more, Joy's fairy palaces.

The Angel spake : " Joy hath her limits set,
    But Sorrow hath no bounds—Joy is a guest
Perchance may enter ; but no heart puls'd yet,
    Where Sorrow did not lay her down to rest ;
She hath no city by so many leagues confin'd,
I cannot measure bounds where there are none to find."

THE CANOE.

My masters twain made me a bed
Of pine-boughs resinous, and cedar ;
Of moss, a soft and gentle breeder
Of dreams of rest ; and me they spread
With furry skins, and laughing said,
" Now she shall lay her polish'd sides,
As queens do rest, or dainty brides,
Our slender lady of the tides !"

My masters twain their camp-soul lit,
Streamed incense from the hissing cones,
Large, crimson flashes grew and whirl'd
Thin, golden nerves of sly light curl'd
Round the dun camp, and rose faint zones,
Half way about each grim bole knit,
Like a shy child that would bedeck
With its soft clasp a Brave's red neck ;
Yet sees the rough shield on his breast,
The awful plumes shake on his crest,
And fearful drops his timid face,
Nor dares complete the sweet embrace.

Into the hollow hearts of brakes,
Yet warm from sides of does and stags,
Pass'd to the crisp dark river flags ;
Sinuous, red as copper snakes,
Sharp-headed serpents, made of light,
Glided and hid themselves in night.

THE CANOE.

My masters twain, the slaughter'd deer
Hung on fork'd boughs—with thongs of leather.
Bound were his stiff, slim feet together—
His eyes like dead stars cold and drear;
The wand'ring firelight drew near
And laid its wide palm, red and anxious,
On the sharp splendor of his branches;
On the white foam grown hard and sere
    On flank and shoulder.
Death—hard as breast of granite boulder,
    And under his lashes
Peer'd thro' his eyes at his life's grey ashes.

My masters twain sang songs that wove
(As they burnish'd hunting blade and rifle)
A golden thread with a cobweb trifle—
Loud of the chase, and low of love.

"O Love, art thou a silver fish?
Shy of the line and shy of gaffing,
Which we do follow, fierce, yet laughing,
Casting at thee the light-wing'd wish,
And at the last shall we bring thee up
From the crystal darkness under the cup
    Of lily folden,
    On broad leaves golden?

"O Love! art thou a silver deer,
Swift thy starr'd feet as wing of swallow,
While we with rushing arrows follow;
And at the last shall we draw near,
And over thy velvet neck cast thongs—
Woven of roses, of stars, of songs?

New chains all moulden
Of rare gems olden !"

They hung the slaughter'd fish like swords
On saplings slender—like scimitars
Bright, and ruddied from new-dead wars,
Blaz'd in the light—the scaly hordes.

They pil'd up boughs beneath the trees,
Of cedar-web and green fir tassel ;
Low did the pointed pine tops rustle,
The camp fire blush'd to the tender breeze.

The hounds laid dew-laps on the ground,
With needles of pine sweet, soft and rusty—
Dream'd of the dead stag stout and lusty ;
A bat by the red flames wove its round.

The darkness built its wigwam walls
Close round the camp, and at its curtain
Press'd shapes, thin woven and uncertain,
As white locks of tall waterfalls.

"MY AIN BONNIE LASS O' THE GLEN."

Ae blink o' the bonnie new mune,
 Ay tinted as sune as she's seen,
Wad licht me to Meg frae the toun,
 Tho' mony the brae-side between :

Ae fuff o' the saftest o' win's,
  As wilyart it kisses the thorn,
Wad blaw me o'er knaggies an' linns—
  To Meg by the side o' the burn!

My daddie's a laird wi' a ha';
  My mither had kin at the court;
I maunna gang wooin' ava'—
  Or ony sic frolicsome sport.
Gin I'd wed—there's a winnock kept bye,
  Wi' bodles an' gear i' her loof—
Gin ony tak her an' her kye,
  He'll glunsh at himsel' for a coof!

My daddie's na doylt, tho' he's auld,
  The winnock is pawkie an' gleg;
When the lammies are pit i' the fauld,
  They're fear'd that I'm aff to my Meg.
My mither sits spinnin'—ae blink
  O' a smile in her kind, bonnie 'ee;
She's minded o' mony a link
  She, stowlins, took o'er the lea

To meet wi' my daddie himsel',
  Tentie jinkin' by lea an' by shaw;
She fu's up his pipe then hersel',
  So I may steal cannie awa'.
O leeze me o' gowany swaird,
  An' the blink o' the bonnie new mune!
An' the cowt stown out o' the yaird
  That trots like a burnie in June!

My Meg she is waitin' abeigh—
    Ilk spunkie that flits through the fen
Wad jealously lead me astray
    Frae my ain bonnie lass o' the glen !
My forbears may groan i' the mools,
    My daddie look dour an' din ;
Wee Love is the callant wha rules,
    An' my Meg is the wifie I'll win !

THE WHITE BULL.

Ev'ry dusk eye in Madrid,
Flash'd blue 'neath its lid ;
As the cry and the clamour ran round,
" The king has been crown'd !
And the brow of his bride has been bound
With the crown of a queen !"
    And between
Te Deum and salvo, the roar
    Of the crowd in the square,
Shook tower and bastion and door,
And the marble of altar and floor ;
    And high in the air,
The wreaths of the incense were driven
To and fro, as are riven
The leaves of a lily, and cast
By the jubilant shout of the blast
    To and fro, to and fro,

And they fell in the chancel and nave,
As the lily falls back on the wave,
And trembl'd and faded and died,
As the white petals tremble and shiver,
    And fade in the tide
Of the jewel dark breast of the river.

" Ho, gossips, the wonderful news !
I have worn two holes in my shoes,
    With the race I have run ;
And, like an old grape in the sun,
I am shrivell'd with drought, for I ran
Like an antelope rather than man.
Our King is a king of Spaniards indeed,
And he loves to see the bold bull bleed ;
And the Queen is a queen, by the saints right fit,
In half of the Spanish throne to sit ;
Tho' blue her eyes and wanly fair,
Her cheek, and her neck, and her flaxen hair ;
    For free and full—
She can laugh as she watches the staggering bull ;
And tap on the jewels of her fan,
    While horse and man,
Reel on in a ruby rain of gore ;
And pout her lip at the Toreador ;
    And fling a jest
If he leave the fight with unsullied vest,
    No crack on his skin,
Where the bull's sharp horn has entered in.
Caramba, gossips, I would not be king,
    And rule and reign
Over wine-shop, and palace, and all broad Spain,

THE WHITE BULL.

If under my wing—
I had not a mate who could joy to the full,
In the gallant death of a man or a bull!"

"What is the news
That has worn two holes in my Saints'-day shoes,
And parch'd me so with heat and speed,
That a skin of wine down my throat must bleed?
Why this, there's a handsome Hidalgo at Court,
And half in sport,
He scour'd the country far and wide,
For a gift to pleasure the royal bride;
And on the broad plains of the Guadalquiver
He gave a pull—
To the jewell'd bridle and silken rein,
That made his stout horse rear and shiver;
For in the dusk reeds of the silver river—
Like the angry stars that redly fly
From the dark blue peaks of the midnight sky,
And smouldering lie,
Blood-red till they die
In the blistering ground—the eyes he saw
Of a bull without blemish, or speck, or flaw,
And a hide as white as a dead saint's soul—
With many a clinking of red pistole;
And draughts of sour wine from the herdsman's bowl,
He paid the full
Price in bright gold of the brave white bull.

"Comrades we all
From the pulpit tall
Have heard the fat friars say God has decreed

That the peasant shall sweat and the soldier shall
    And Hidalgo and King   [bleed,
    May righteously wring
Sweat and blood from us all, weak, strong, young
And turn the tax into Treasury gold.   [and old,
Well, the friar knows best,
    Or why wear a cowl?
    And a cord round his breast?
    So why should we scowl?
The friar is learned and knows the mind,
    From core to rind,
Of God, and the Virgin, and ev'ry saint
That a tongue can name or a brush can paint;
    And I've heard him declare—
With a shout that shook all the birds in the air,
    That two kinds of clay
Are used in God's Pottery every day.
The finest and best he puts in a mould
    Of purest gold,
Stamped with the mark of His signet ring,
    And He turns them out,
    (While the angels shout)
The Pope and the priest, the Hidalgo and King!
And He gives them dominion full and just
O'er the creatures He kneads from the common dust,
And the clay, stamped with His proper sign,
    Has right divine
To the sweat, and the blood and the bended knee
Of such, my gossips, as ye and me.
    Who cares? Not I
Only let King and Hidalgo buy,

THE WHITE BULL.

With the red pistoles
They wring from our sweltering bodies and souls,
   Treasures as full
Of the worth of gold as the bold white bull !

" The Hidalgo rode back to the Court :
   And to finish the sport,
   When the King had been crowned,
And the flaxen hair of the bride had been bound.
   With the crown of the Queen ;
He took a huge necklace of plates of gold,
   With rubies between ;
   And wound it threefold
Round the brute's broad neck, and with ruby ring
In its fire-puffed nostrils had it led
To the feet of the Queen as she sat by the King,
With the red crown set on her lily head ;
   And she said—
' Let the bull be led
To the floor
   Of the arena : Proclaim,
   In my name,
That the valliant and bold Toreador,
   Who slays him shall pull
The rubies and gold from the gore
   Of the bold white bull !'

" That is the news which I bear ;
I heard it below in the square—
   And to and fro,
   I heard the voice blow
Of Pedro, the brawny young Toreador,

THE WHITE BULL.

As he swore
By the tremulous light of the golden star
That quivers beneath the soft lid
    Of Pilar,
Who sells tall lilies through fair Madrid ;
    He would wind six-fold
Round her neck, long, slender, round and full,
    The rubies and gold
    That three times rolled
Round the mighty breast of the bold white bull.
    And loudly he sang,
    While the wine cups rang,
        ' If I'm the bravest Toreador
            In gallant, gay Madrid,
        If thou hast got the brightest eye
            That dances 'neath a lid ;
        If e'er of Andalusian wine
            I drank a bottle full,
        The gold, the rubies shall be thine
            That deck the bold white bull.'

" Already a chorus rings out in the city,
    A jubilant ditty,
    And every guitar
Vibrates to the names of Pedro and Pilar ;
And the strings and voices are soulless and dull
That sound not the name of the bold white bull !"

MARCH.

Shall Thor with his hammer
  Beat on the mountain,
As on an anvil,
  A shackle and fetter?

Shall the lame Vulcan
  Shout as he swingeth
God-like his hammer,
  And forge thee a fetter?

Shall Jove, the Thunderer,
  Twine his swift lightnings
With his loud thunders,
  And forge thee a shackle?

" No," shouts the Titan,
  The young lion-throated;
" Thor, Vulcan, nor Jove
  Cannot shackle and bind me."

Tell what will bind thee,
  Thou young world-shaker,
Up vault our oceans,
  Down fall our forests.

Ship-masts and pillars
  Stagger and tremble,
Like reeds by the margins
  Of swift running waters.

Men's hearts at thy roaring
    Quiver like harebells
Smitten by hailstones,
    Smitten and shaken.

" O sages and wise men !
    O bird-hearted tremblers !
Come, I will show ye
    A shackle to bind me.

I, the lion-throated,
    The shaker of mountains !
I, the invincible,
    Lasher of oceans !

Past the horizon,
    Its ring of pale azure
Past the horizon,
    Where scurry the white clouds,

There are buds and small flowers—
    Flowers like snow-flakes,
Blossoms like rain-drops,
    So small and tremulous.

These in a fetter
    Shall shackle and bind me,
Shall weigh down my shouting
    With their delicate perfume !"

But who this frail fetter
    Shall forge on an anvil,
With hammer of feather
    And anvil of velvet ?

"Past the horizon,
  In the palm of a valley,
Her feet in the grasses,
  There is a maiden.

She smiles on the flowers,
  They widen and redden;
She weeps on the flowers,
  They grow up and kiss her.

She breathes in their bosoms,
  They breathe back in odours;
Inarticulate homage,
  Dumb adoration.

She shall wreathe them in shackles,
  Shall weave them in fetters;
In chains shall she braid them,
  And me shall she fetter.

I, the invincible;
  March, the earth-shaker;
March, the sea-lifter;
  March, the sky-render;

March, the lion-throated.
  April the weaver
Of delicate blossoms,
  And moulder of red buds—

Shall, at the horizon,
  Its ring of pale azure,
Its scurry of white clouds,
  Meet in the sunlight."

"THE EARTH WAXETH OLD."

When yellow-lock'd and crystal ey'd
   I dream'd green woods among ;
Where tall trees wav'd from side to side,
And in their green breasts deep and wide,
I saw the building blue jay hide,
   O, then the earth was young !

The winds were fresh and brave and bold,
   The red sun round and strong ;
No prophet voice chill, loud and cold,
Across my woodland dreamings roll'd,
" The green earth waxeth sere and old,
   That once was fair and young !"

I saw in scarr'd and knotty bole,
   The fresh'ning of the sap ;
When timid spring gave first small dole,
Of sunbeams thro' bare boughs that stole,
I saw the bright'ning blossoms roll,
   From summer's high pil'd lap.

And where an ancient oak tree lay
   The forest stream across,
I mus'd above the sweet shrill spray,
I watch'd the speckl'd trout at play,
I saw the shadows dance and sway
   On ripple and on moss.

"THE EARTH WAXETH OLD."

I pull'd the chestnut branches low,
    As o'er the stream they hung,
To see their bursting buds of snow—
I heard the sweet spring waters flow—
My heart and I we did not know
    But that the earth was young!

I joy'd in solemn woods to see,
    Where sudden sunbeams clung,
On open space of mossy lea,
The violet and anemone,
Wave their frail heads and beckon me—
    Sure then the earth was young!

I heard the fresh wild breezes birr,
    New budded boughs among,
I saw the deeper tinting stir
In the green tassels of the fir,
I heard the pheasant rise and whirr,
    Above her callow young.

I saw the tall fresh ferns prest,
    By scudding doe and fawn;
I say the grey dove's swelling breast,
Above the margin of her nest;
When north and south and east and west
    Roll'd all the red of dawn.

At eventide at length I lay,
    On grassy pillow flung;
I saw the parting bark of day,
With crimson sails and shrouds all gay,
With golden fires drift away,
    The billowy clouds among.

I saw the stately planets sail
On that blue ocean wide ;
I saw blown by some mystic gale,
Like silver ship in elfin tale,
That bore some damsel rare and pale,
The moon's slim crescent glide.

And ev'ry throb of spring that shook
The rust'ling boughs among,
That filled the silver vein of brook,
That lit with bloom the mossy nook,
Cried to my boyish bosom :   " Look !
How fresh the earth and young !"

The winds were fresh, the days as clear
As crystals set in gold.
No shape, with prophet-mantle drear,
Thro' those old woods came drifting near,
To whisper in my wond'ring ear,
" The green earth waxeth old."

"THE WISHING STAR."

Day floated down the sky ; a perfect day,
Leaving a footprint of pale primrose gold
Along the west, that when her lover, Night,
Fled with his starry lances in pursuit,
Across the sky, the way she went might shew.
From the faint ting'd ridges of the sea, the Moon

Sprang up like Aphrodite from the wave,
Which as she climb'd the sky still held
Her golden tresses to its swelling breast,
Where wide dispread their quiv'ring glories lay,
(Or as the shield of night, full disk'd and red,
As flowers that look forever towards the Sun),
A terrace with a fountain and an oak
Look'd out upon the sea : The fountain danced
Beside the huge old tree as some slim nymph,
Rob'd in light silver might her frolics shew
Before some hoary king, while high above,
He shook his wild, long locks upon the breeze—
And sigh'd deep sighs of " All is vanity !"
Behind, a wall of Norman William's time
Rose mellow, hung with ivy, here and there
Torn wide apart to lèt a casement peer
Upon the terrace. On a carv'd sill I leant
(A fleur-de-lis bound with an English rose)
And look'd above me into two such eyes
As would have dazzl'd from that ancient page
That new old cry that hearts so often write
In their own ashes, " All is vanity !"
" Know'st thou—" she said, with tender eyes far-fix'd,
On the wide arch that domes our little earth,
" That when a star hurls on with shining wings,
" On some swift message from his throne of light,
" The ready heart may wish, and the ripe fruit—
" Fulfilment—drop into the eager palm ?"
" Then let us watch for such a star," quoth I.
" Nay, love," she said, " 'Tis but an idle tale."
But some swift feeling smote upon her brow

A rosy shadow. I turn'd and watch'd the sky—
Calmly the cohorts of the night swept on,
Led by the wide-wing'd vesper; and against the moon
Where low her globe trembl'd upon the edge
Of the wide amethyst that clearly paved
The dreamy sapphire of the night, there lay
The jetty spars of some tall ship, that look'd
The night's device upon his ripe-red shield.
And suddenly down towards the moon there ran—
From some high space deep-veil'd in solemn blue,
A little star, a point of trembling gold,
Gone swift as seen. "My wishing-star," quoth I,
" Shall tell my wish? Did'st note that little star?
" Its brightness died not, it but disappeared,
" To whirl undim'd thro' space. I wish'd our love
" Might blot the 'All is vanity' from this brief life,
" Burning brightly as that star and winging on
" Thro' unseen space of veil'd Eternity,
" Brightened by Immortality—not lost."
" Awful and sweet the wish !" she said, and so—
We rested in the silence of content.

HOW DEACON FRY BOUGHT A " DUCHESS."

It sorter skeer'd the neighbours round,
    For of all the 'tarnal set thet clutches
Their dollars firm, he wus the boss;
    An' yet he went and byed a " Duchess."

I never will forget the day
   He druv her from the city market;
I guess thar warn't more'n two
   Thet stayed to hum thet day in Clarket.

And one of them wus Gran'pa Finch,
   Who's bed-rid up to Spense's attic :
The other Aunt Mehitabel,
   Whose jints and temper is rheumatic.
She said she "guessed that Deacon Fry
   Would some day see he'd done more fitter
To send his dollars savin' souls
   Than waste 'em on a horn'd critter !"

We all turn'd out at Pewse's store,
   The last one jest inside the village ;
The Jedge he even chanc'd along,
   And so did good old Elder Millage.
We sot around on kegs and planks,
   And on the fence we loung'd precarious;
The Elder felt to speak a word,
   And sed his thoughts wus very various.

He sed the Deacon call'd to mind
   The blessed patriarchs and their cattle ;
" To whose herds cum a great increase
   When they in furrin parts did settle."
We nodded all our skulls at this,
   But Argue Bill he rapped his crutches ;
Sed he, " I guess they never paid
   Five hundred dollars for a ' Duchess.'"

Bill and the Elder allers froze
    To subjects sorter disputatious,
So on the 'lasses keg they sot,
    And had an argue fair and spacious.
Good land! when Solon cum in sight,
    By lawyer Smithett's row o' beeches;
His black span seemed to crawl along
    Ez slow ez Dr. Jones's leeches.

Sez Sister Fry, who was along,
    " I sorter think my specs is muggy;
" But Solon started out from hum
    " This mornin' in the new top buggy.
" Jeddiah rid old chestnut Jim,
    " An' Sammy rid the roan filly;
" I told 'em when they started off
    " It looked redikless, soft and silly,

" To see three able-bodied men
    " An' four stout horses drive one critter;
" O land o' song! will some one look?
    " From hed to foot I'm in a twitter."
Wal, up we swarm'd on Pewse's fence,
    And Bill he histed on his crutches;
We all was curus to behold
    The Deac's five hundred dollar " Duchess."

I've heerd filosofurs declar,
    This life be's kind o' snarly jinted;
And every human standin' thar
    Felt sorter gin'ral disappointed.

What sort o' crazy animile
Hed got the Deacon in its clutches?
They cum along in spankin' style—
Old Solon and his sons and " Duchess."

Her heels wus up, her hed wus down,
An or'nary cross-gritted critter
As ever browsed around the town,
And kept the women folks a-twitter,
A-boostin' up the garding rails,
And browsin' on the factory bleachin',
And kickin' up the milkin' pails :
Bill he riz up, ez true ez preachin'.

Sez he, excited like, " I'll 'low,
To swaller both these here old crutches—
Ef thet ain't Farmer Slyby's cow,
Old Bossie turn'd inter a " Duchess !"
Wal, 'twus k'rect ! The Deacon swore
Some hefty swars and sot the clutches
Of law to work ; but seed no more
The chap thet sold him thet thar " Duchess."

MY IRISH LOVE.

Beside the saffron of a curtain, lit
With broidered flowers, below a golden fringe
That on her silver shoulder made a glow,
Like the sun kissing lilies in the dawn ;
She sat—my Irish love—slim, light and tall.
Between his mighty paws her stag-hound held,
(Love-jealous he) the foam of her pale robes,
Rare laces of her land, and his red eyes,
Half lov'd me, grown familiar at her side,
Half pierc'd me, doubting my soul's right to stand
His lady's wooer in the courts of Love.
Above her, knitted silver, fell a web
Of light from waxen tapers slipping down,
First to the wide-winged star of em'ralds set
On the black crown with its blue burnish'd points
Of raven light ; thence, fonder, to the cheek
O'er which flew drifts of rose-leaves wild and rich,
With lilied pauses in the wine-red flight ;
For when I whisper'd, like a wind in June,
My whisper toss'd the roses to and fro
In her dear face, and when I paus'd they lay

Still in her heart. Then lower fell the light.
A silver chisel cutting the round arm
Clear from the gloom ; and dropped like dew
On the crisp lily, di'mond clasp'd, that lay
In happy kinship on her pure, proud breast,
And thence it sprang like Cupid, nimble-wing'd,
To the quaint love-ring on her finger bound
And set it blazing like a watch-fire, lit
To guard a treasure. Then up sprang the flame
Mad for her eyes, but those grey worlds were deep
In seas of native light : and when I spoke
They wander'd shining to the shining moon
That gaz'd at us between the parted folds
Of yellow, rich with gold and daffodils,
Dropping her silver cloak on Innisfail.
O worlds, those eyes ! there Laughter lightly toss'd
His gleaming cymbals ; Large and most divine.
Pity stood in their crystal doors with hands
All generous outspread ; in their pure depths
Mov'd Modesty, chaste goddess, snow-white of brow,
And shining, vestal limbs ; rose-fronted stood
Blushing, yet strong ; young Courage, knightly in
His virgin arms, and simple, russet Truth
Play'd like a child amongst her tender thoughts—
Thoughts white as daisies snow'd upon the lawn.

Unheeded, Dante on the cushion lay,
His golden clasps yet lock'd—no poet tells
The tale of Love with such a wizard tongue
That lovers slight dear Love himself to list.

Our wedding eve, and I had brought to her
The jewels of my house new set for her
(As I did set the immemorial pearl
Of our old honour in the virgin gold
Of her high soul) with grave and well pleased eyes,
And critic lips, and kissing finger tips,
She prais'd the bright tiara and its train
Of lesser splendours—nor blush'd nor smil'd :
They were but fitting pages to her state,
And had no tongues to speak between our souls.

But I would have her smile ripe for me then,
Swift treasure of a moment—so I laid
Between her palms a little simple thing,
A golden heart, grav'd with my name alone,
And round it, twining close, small shamrocks link'd
Of gold, mere gold : no jewels made it rich,
Until twin di'monds shatter'd from her eyes
And made the red gold rare. "True Knight," she said,
" Your English heart with Irish shamrocks bound !"
" A golden prophet of eternal truth,"
I said, and kissed the roses of her palms,
And then the shy, bright roses of her lips,
And all the jealous jewels shone forgot
In necklace and tiara, as I clasp'd
The gold heart and its shamrocks round her neck.
My fair, pure soul ! My noble Irish love !

A HUNGRY DAY.

I mind him well, he was a quare ould chap,
    Come like meself from swate ould Erin's sod,
He hired me wanst to help his harvest in ;
    The crops was fine that summer, prais'd be God !
He found us, Rosie, Mickie, an' meself,
    Just landed in the emigration shed,
Meself was tyin' on there bits of clothes,
    Their mother (rest her tender sowl !) was dead.

It's not meself can say of what she died ;
    But t'was the year the praties felt the rain,
And rotted in the soil ; an' just to dhraw
    The breath of life was one long hungry pain.
If we were haythens in a furrin' land,
    Not in a country grand in Christian pride,
Faith, then a man might have the face to say
    'Twas of stharvation my poor Shylie died.

But whin the parish docthor come at last,
    Whin death was like a sun-burst in her eyes,
(They looked straight into heaven) an her ears
    Wor deaf to the poor childer's hungry cries ;
He touched the bones stretched on the mouldy sthraw ;
    "She's gone !" he says, and drew a solemn frown ;
"I fear, my man, she's dead." "Of what ?" says I.
    He coughed, and says, "She's let her system down !"

"An' that's God's truth!" says I, an' felt about
   To touch her dawney hand, for all looked dark,
An' in my hunger-bleached, shmall-beatin' heart,
   I felt the kindlin' of a burning spark.
" O, by me sowl, that is the holy truth !
   There's Rosie's cheek has kept a dimple still,
An' Mickie's eyes are, bright—the craythur there
   Died that the weeny ones might eat there fill."

An' whin they spread the daisies thick and white,
   Above her head that wanst lay on my breast,
I had no tears, but took the childhers' hands,
   An' says, " We'll lave the mother to her rest,"
An' och! the sod was green that summers day ;
   An' rainbows crossed the low hills, blue an' fair ;
But black an' foul the blighted furrows stretched,
   An' sent their cruel poison through the air.

An' all was quiet—on the sunny sides
   Of hedge an' ditch the stharvin' craythurs lay,
An' thim as lack'd the rint from empty walls
   Of little cabins, wapin' turned away.
God's curse lay heavy on the poor ould sod,
   An' whin upon her increase His right hand
Fell with'ringly, there samed no bit of blue
   For Hope to shine through on the sthricken land.

No facthory chimblys shmoked agin the sky,
   No mines yawn'd on the hills so full an' rich ;
A man whose praties failed had nought to do,
   But fold his hands an' die down in a ditch !

A flame rose up widin me feeble heart,
  Whin passin' through me cabin's hingeless dure,
I saw the mark of Shylie's coffin in
  The grey dust on the empty earthen flure.

I lifted Rosie's face betwixt me hands;
  Says I, 'Me girleen, you an' Mick an' me,
Must lave the green ould sod, an' look for food
  In thim strange countries far beyant the sea."
An' so it chanced, when landed on the streets,
  Ould Dolan, rowlin' a quare ould shay,
Came there to hire a man to save his whate,
  An' hired meself and Mickie by the day.

"An' bring the girleen, Pat," he says, an' looked
  At Rosie lanin' up agin me knee;
"The wife will be right plaised to see the child,
  The weeney shamrock from beyant the sea.
We've got a tidy place, the saints be praised!
  As nice a farm as ever brogan trod,
A hundred acres—us as never owned
  Land big enough to make a lark a sod!"

"Bedad," sez I, "I heerd them over there
  Tell how the goold was lyin' in the sthreet,
An' guineas in the very mud that sthuck
  To the ould brogans on a poor man's feet!"
"Begorra, Pat," says Dolan, "may ould Nick
  Fly off wid thim rapscallions, schaming rogues,
An' sind thim thrampin' purgatory's flure,
  Wid red hot guineas in their polished brogues!"

A HUNGRY DAY.

"Och, thin," says I, "meself agrees to that!"
  Ould Dolan smiled wid eyes so bright an' grey;
Says he "Kape up yer heart—I never knew
  Since I come out a single hungry day!"

"But thin I left the crowded city sthreets,
  There men galore to toil in thim an' die,
Meself wint wid me axe to cut a home
  I·   n woods beneath the clear, swate sky.

"I did that same: an' God be prais'd this day!
  Plenty sits smilin' by me own dear dure:
An' in them years I never wanst have seen
  A famished child creep tremblin' on me flure!"

I listened to ould Dolan's honest words,
  That's twenty years ago this very spring,
An' Mick is married—an' me Rosie wears
  A swateheart's little, shinin' goulden ring.

'Twould make yer heart lape just to take a look
  At the green fields upon me own big farm;
An' God be prais'd! all men may have the same
  That owns an axe! an' has a strong right arm!

LaVergne, TN USA
02 November 2010
203093LV00016B/13/P